'We spend our tir
rationally to a world which we
understand and recognise, but
which no longer exists.'

Eddie Obeng

# Who Killed the Sparq?

# THE NEWWORLD™ BOOK SERIES

# Who Killed the Sparq?

From Smart-Failure to Transformation

*Eddie Obeng*

*WhoKilledTheSparq.com*

**Printed on recycled paper**

First published 2013 by **London Business Press** in association with PentacleWorks The Virtual Media Company

A CIP catalogue record for this book is available from the British Library

ISBN 978-1-909877-00-9 (paperback)   ISBN 978-1-909877-01-6 (ebook)
ISBN 978-1-909877-02-3 (ebook)       ISBN 978-1-909877-03-0 (ebook)

# Contents

## How to Use this Book

This book is in three parts.

**The Suspects:** These are short chapters written from different points of view from across an enterprise.

At the end of each chapter you need to pause and decide if this suspect is the guilty one. What clues have you spotted that incriminate them? Is there any evidence? Or is this person merely an accessory?

Join the discussion and add your sleuth-like views at:
✹ http://WhoKilledTheSparq.com

**The Culprit:** This section begins by inviting you to take a HealthCheck. Once you have your results you will know which cards form our deck you need to play. There are weblinks ✹ on the cards to more information and guidance. You will find a selection of ideas and tools useful in tracking down and removing the barriers *you* have to innovation.

**The Evidence:** This is an invitation to join a global community of innovators who meet to discuss and share innovation concepts ideas on ♣ QUBE.

Much more…

As you go through the book you will find hypertext links to other parts of the book and in addition some special icons for links.

| | | | |
|---|---|---|---|
| ♣ | Access to QUBE | ▬ | Tools and techniques |
| ♟ | Explanatory videos | ✹ | Web pages |
| ◉ | Photograph for context | Words | Links to more information and explanations of words or phrases (the book is written in English English) |

At any time you can enter the *qubicles* where much of the action in the book takes place. Invite a couple of your colleagues to join you in the qubicle and try out some of the tools and techniques together.

Project qubicle here: ♣

Innovation Workshop Qubicle here: ♣

♣Access to QUBE:

Your user name is: me<use a number from 1 to 100>@ALCORP.com

For example: me57@alcorp.com

Your password is Sparq. <capital S>

Join the WAM innovation community in hub-Q. Apply for an entry pass and get details of the amazing 'Introductory Offer'! http://hub-Q.com

Enjoy the book and all the links.

## Author's Introduction

I love ideas. I hate ideas. All my life I've found it easy to come up with ideas. I love the way ideas open up possibilities almost like magic, making things seem possible which weren't before.

But I hate the obligation they put you under. I hate the fact that they commit you to and pre-determine what you are going to be doing with your life for some time. And finally I really hate it when the idea isn't 'just right' and ends up too difficult to execute or not quite capturing my or other people's imagination.

During my career I've been lucky enough to innovate. I designed Europe's most energy-efficient vegetable oil refinery in Purfleet UK for Unilever. I invented and patented a biologically based sour gas treatment system for Shell. I broke the one-size-fits-all, 3-sessions-a-day mould for courses at Ashridge, enabling individual tailoring based on needs and competences and a minute-by-minute flexible timetable. I managed to improve Ashridge's profitability by developing an effective way of making sure that the best tutors got the credit for doing the most difficult work. I invented and run a virtual business school, numerous sessions, exercises and learning journeys.

One invention that got away and has upset me to this day is my invention of the transparent window on the side of kettles. Whilst I was doing a PhD in Biotechnology in the 80s, I picked up the job of running our coffee room. Before I took over, the club would often run out of money and coffee. So when I took over I began to **observe** everything – I found out how many cups of coffee you could make from a jar. How much milk was used at the start or end of the week. How long it took the water to boil – this had an impact on how long the queue for coffee would be and therefore how many biscuits you could sell to people waiting in the queue. And 🎥 I observed that there was always a 'waste of time' as each individual had to remove the lid of the kettle (or lift and weigh it by hand) to check if there was enough water in it for the drinks they wanted to make. I realised what the solution should be – a 'sight glass'. A sight glass is a long glass tube which runs vertically on the outside of an opaque steel vessel the level of the liquid in the glass is the same as the level in the vessel. One coffee break I proposed a solution – a solution to a problem that the consumers were unaware they had – that I drill a hole in the kettle and install a sight glass so that we would know instantly how much water was left in the kettle. My idea was greeted by tremendous howls of derisive laughter, especially by Nigel, my best friend. I was cowed and embarrassed and did nothing about it. Three years later Swan launched a plastic kettle with a 'sight glass' containing a small floating red ball. Designed by Richard Seymour, it was a tremendous success **and I kicked myself for not having the courage** of my convictions, for exposing my poor helpless idea to such strong criticism by **sharing my vision instead of creating a shared vision**, for not having the **presence of mind** to have put forward or at least done a patent search.

# This book is dedicated to my good friend and inspiration,

# Jacques Racloz

## From your 'Professor'

It was in 1995 that I first met Jacques Racloz.

I'd been working with Justin van Gennep and Jeanette Swan and their organisation had decided to reenergise itself with an initiative called Taking the Initiative (TTI)

I met Jacques at a hotel in Surrey for lunch and to discuss how I could help with the initiative. As I waited, in came this tall handsome man with a large bushy beard wearing a cravat and with the downward handshake of a bear. Very, very scary. Fortunately I don't believe in first impressions and by the end of our lunch together we had hit it off.

The innovation which Jacques' team and I went on to create was originally named the Operational Grid. It was the first execution of a virtual organisation within the global pharmaceutical industry. 🎥 The implementation shortened the time to market for new offers, improved the focus on the customer and market, enabled outsourcing of certain services, improved the margins of the organisation through the new money-making process and did many more things. Jacques even led his team to lay out the UK offices in the style of the virtual organisation, colour coding the departments and issuing T-shirts so people could be identified and connect to the right stakeholders. It was a very exciting and profitable project and even influenced the organisation design of the merged Sandoz and Ciba organisation to form the largest pharmaceutical company on the planet at the time.

It is to Jacques that I dedicate this book.

---

## About the Author

# Eddie Obeng

Eddie is Learning Director of Pentacle The Virtual Business School (Founded 1994). He was previously an Executive Director at Ashridge Management College, having begun his career with Shell.

*An agent provocateur* **Financial Times**

*Our resident guru* **Project Manager Today**

Unusual as an academic to back his ideas with his own money **The Sunday Times**

A 'leading revolutionary' **Financial Times**

Eddie Obeng on TED

Eddie Obeng on LinkedIn

Eddie Obeng on QUBE

Eddie Obeng on Twitter

Eddie Obeng's Blog

More from EddieObeng.com

More on Eddie Obeng's philosophy from WorldAfterMidnight.com

More from Eddie Obeng at Pentacle The Virtual Business School

Thanks to the Pentacle Team, especially Susan Ross, David Lomas, Christophe Gillet and Andy Burnett.

# PART ONE:
# THE SUSPECTS

> *'Some people see things that are and ask, Why?*
> *Some people dream of things that never were and ask, Why not?*
> *Some people have to go to work and don't have time for all that...'*
> George Carlin

## Chapter 1   The SUSPECT: Chief Executive Officer

## The End

'Dead.' His head drops dejectedly into his hands and he rubs his eyes with his palms. 'Murdered. Somehow...' his voice trails off. The summer evening has now turned to dark night in the window behind him. He sits facing into the room towards the door at a large oak desk, his face coloured a jaundiced yellow by the desk lamp. In front of him on the desk is a hand-crafted, African Blackwood name plaque which proclaims in gold letters that this is John Troy CEO.

In front of John is a report. A consultants' report on the synergies which would be gained as a result of a merger between his company and their fiercest competitor. At over five hundred bucks per page John should be riveted, caught up in the detail and arguments. Instead he whispers to himself softly, 'I'm sure I've read this paragraph on debt restructuring before,' which he has. And then unexpectedly he says out loud mournfully, 'Definitely dead. Shame I...' his voice trails off. Now he's lost in unhappy thoughts. 'I'm in big trouble. I promised **Them** that there would be a result, a big result, a result to show that we could take on the global challenge of low price labour and win. But our most promising opportunity is dead, stone dead. Dead. Dead like a parrot,' he thinks, allowing himself a wry,

3

lopsided smile. Then loudly, reproaching himself, he adds, 'I should never have got so carried away. I mean, everyone in the sector is struggling with innovation. Why did I have to promise **Them** double digit growth through sustainable growth, through innovation?' John knows the reason he promised double digit growth. It was simply because the private equity guys had been sniffing around and he knew what that meant. He shudders. He really is at his wits end. He's done everything he can think of and a lot more besides, he recalls. He's set innovation as a KPI linked to bonuses, he's hired the 'best' consultants, McKlaskeys, whose claim, plastered all over every international airport, is that they *'Make Innovation Happen'*; well they'd better, for what they charge a day! John needs to roll-out an innovation strategy across the organisation. But he doesn't want to fly all his global executives or hundreds of managers to a summit at great expense, explain it to them and then have them go back home, back to their old ways. 'I need to make sure that they learn new ways of working, collaborate in delivery around the globe, and I need to be involved with what is happening.' He pauses, reflecting on time, costs and the difficulty of this. What he needed was… He's stumped. What other choices did he have? He'd gone all modern and trendy and started a blog and his comms people regularly tweeted quotes from him on his behalf about how crucial innovation was. But this had little effect. He'd appointed a Director of Innovation. Another pause, auditing his actions and then he is suddenly pleased with himself that he has covered everything practical, and then reflects, 'What a shame the guy leading their best innovation opportunity has just quit.' John broods darkly. To be honest, he'd never really liked Mark. 'Mark was never straight. Always smug, some sort of joke no one else ever got. Wouldn't stick to the processes. I mean how could you trust a guy like that? You never knew where you were with him, always coming up with something new and different from what had been agreed at the last meeting!' **A successful organisation needed clear accountability and control** – the problem with these creative types was you couldn't control them and John desperately needed absolute control at all times. 'And that crazy idea of Mark's to scrap the Key Performance Indicators and allow people to have some flexibility with their time. Madness. Without checking the billable hours, the sales targets and making sure people delivered their projects exactly when they promised – not a day early/not a day late, all hell could break loose.' John stands up, turns sharply to the right and stares blankly out of the window, into the void of blackness. He stares at nothing, just feeling the fear and melancholy of his soul. His body mirrors his mood with hunched shoulders and motionless arms. He'd wanted more certainty, more control. After all, it was his neck on the line. And now this... 'It's dead. I need something else to show, something to parade, a hot, "sexy" product idea, a market opportunity which gives us a head start. And that **must not fail** or "They" will have my head... on a platter.'

He straightens up, the load on his shoulders lifting slightly with a new train of thought: 'I should have some time this weekend to think it over and, well, if we can't get any good growth through our innovations I can always go for a merger. If I get the CEO post in the merged organisation "They'll" have to give me the standard 100 day honeymoon to sort things out, plus **since there is no financial history the analysts won't be able to raise the pressure by comparing performance to the past, for at least a year**. And even if that didn't work we'd be bigger and more dominant in the market. That should help with the performance. If I don't get the top job there are my stock options and the exit bonus I negotiated when I took the job... that should pay for at least 70 feet of yacht...'

*'The dream is real, my friends.*
*The failure to realise it is the only unreality.'*
Toni Cade Bambera

## Chapter 2   THE SUSPECT: Me

# Ideas Lost

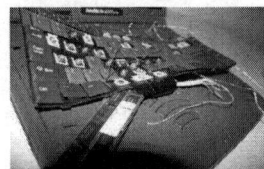 'Should I stay indoors and work or should I go out, enjoy the sunshine, clear my head and perhaps come up with the breakthrough ideas I need to present tomorrow?'

It's ridiculous. It's Sunday. Worse, it's a glorious, warm, blue-sky, Sunday morning and here I am in my study, on my computer, preparing a PowerPoint presentation for Monday's ExCo meeting to explain why, after yet another month, our new *Growth Through Innovation* process has so far failed to get any real results. They've graciously granted me 20 minutes out of a 5 hour meeting. Strange how, for an organisation which claims that *'Innovation is our life-blood'* on this year's annual report, our board actually dedicates so little time to helping the blood to flow freely.

I reach for my cup of coffee. It's very bitter, but worse, it's gone cold. 'I wish someone would invent a "self-hot-keeping" cup. I'd buy it,' I say in a frustrated voice out loud to myself. So back to my GTI presentation. It's three months since I was asked by John Troy to 'lead our organisation's transformation to deliver real growth by becoming the most innovative company in our sector.' The truth is that after years of growing by acquiring other companies and really stretching to get the most out of our brands, it's becoming clearer and clearer that **our organisation isn't inventing its <u>own</u> future fast enough in what is now a fast-changing and complex business environment.**

This fact has been driven home by two things. First, by what we euphemistically call **the BRIC[1] Wall Challenge, the fact that competition from the East and South is easily matching us on quality of existing products and beating us on price**, and can only get worse as eastern domestic demand grows and provides our new competitors with a solid base. And second, by what we have nicknamed **the Economic Cliff. Not for jumping off but for standing at the bottom of and looking up at the fact that many previously industrialised countries have pre-spent over a decade's worth of future income** – so getting things moving again isn't a mountain to climb, it's a sheer vertical cliff.

I've been working flat out trying to support our growth targets by getting the organisation to innovate. It's a far higher-pressure job than I'd anticipated. Pressure because our CEO has promised our investors that 'our move to *become "the most innovative company in our sector"* is what will fuel substantial double digit real growth.' He made that statement four months ago and now he is getting nervous and twitchy. He knows that in the past the **financial returns from innovation projects haven't been too strong.** We had to scrap our last breakthrough offering last year after two months in the market and it was headline news. Pressure because everyone knows that as a result my predecessor was fired. And now even more pressure. We had only one good chance, our most promising new offer… but now… now that Mark has quit it's probably dead.

The truth is **that most of our people lack the 'can do, especially new' attitude we need** and even where we do have great ideas **we find it really hard to make our great ideas happen.** For example, we came up with a market beater in terms of the customer support system, but guess what? We were third to market. Probably as a result, **people leading any project or change which**

---

1    Brazil, Russia, India, China.

is labelled as 'innovative' change in the organisation, like Mark, end up exposed and lonely.

I haven't been slow to get started. As soon as I took the job I did my homework and John Troy had just appointed the best regarded consultants in the field to establish what we needed to do to make innovation work. They said that what we lacked and needed urgently was a **process for managing innovation**. They explained how, without a systematic process, effort would be unfocused since it was important that people were encouraged to take risks and fail often. They argued articulately that **the more clearly defined and benchmarked the process the better**. The process we've started to implement is based on the analogy of an innovation pipeline. The more ideas we put in which we can sign-off the more results come out. Simple! We've taken their ideas about **divergent and convergent thinking** on board. We've started an **open innovation and user-centred design web presence** and much more. We've set out to **recreate our key internal product development and marketing processes** and we've explored our channel to market. So why is there so little to show? And why is Mark's project dead?

For tomorrow's meeting I'm creating a complex graphic of our 'innovation pipeline process' explaining the **roles and accountabilities, the stage gating process** and the frequency and composition of review board meetings.

We've **run creativity workshops** to get more ideas into the innovation pipeline. But I guess if I'm honest the depressing reality is that nothing 'really good' seems to come out of the workshops. People just end up putting forward the same-old, tired 'hobby horses' they've been banging on about for years. They were bad ideas the first time round and have putrefied with repetition.

The latest trend is that the senior managers announce that they will be joining meetings and workshops, and then pull out of attending at the very last minute because 'There is a very important issue/ meeting/ customer response, etc., which has just come up.' They want to be seen to be supporting the innovation initiative but it seems to me that they sense failure and are unwilling to put any more time into it. 'We need to invest in internal communications to talk up the initiative, but there's no budget for that,' I think downheartedly.

I rise to get a fresh cup of coffee, pausing only to save my work before I set off for the kitchen. I click on File then Save but instead of saving my file the entire screen turns blue and a Warning!!! Flashes up on my screen. It says:

**EXPLODER caused a general protection fault in module USER>EXE at 0004:00005fdd**

I have no idea at all what this means so I hit Esc several times but it's frozen. Somewhere deep inside my chest a scream starts, primeval and throbbing. By the time it reaches my throat it sounds like a bass, grumbling roar. 'Ararrrrghghrgha!' My laptop's crashed and I've lost the last two hours' work. I've lost it all, all my ideas, all my colours.

All the innovation books I've ever read emphasise and re-emphasise the importance of failing, failing often and not being upset but wearing it as a medal of honour of having the right mind-set. Our consultants endorsed that view. Well, my computer's failed so that should be excellent indeed. But I've had enough of failure. I slip on my old deck shoes and in a second I'm out in the garden.

*'In dreams and in love there are no impossibilities.'*
Janos Arany

## Chapter 3   The SUSPECT: Mark

## Who Killed the Sparq?

 In his 'den', the light from a tablet computer showing a film with whites, greens and vivid reds, the only light source in the room, plays on the still features of the man in the armchair. The armchair is old, battered but looks extremely comfortable. Is it this comfort which makes him motionless? He barely seems to be breathing and his eyes, once shiny with energy and wonder, are now only shiny with tears. The next morning, Monday, he would be missed. They would say many things about him. They would say he 'died' of worry. He 'died' of overwork. He'd watched his fellow employees, people he'd worked with for years, turn from friends into colleagues into adversaries, as wave after wave of redundancies and mergers had broken the soul of the company he'd once been proud to work for, and made concepts like 'pride in a job well done' and 'pride in really providing phenomenal service and products' sound dated and out of touch. Finally the vicious cost cutting and headcount reduction had got to him – not directly but through the project he'd put so much of his dreams into. In the end it had all seemed pointless, the daily strain of striving to be the 'last man standing', in the modern era's corporate version of 'The Weakest link', keeping your head down to top up your pension, which probably wouldn't be worth as much as you had hoped.

There had to be more to work than that. More to it than exchanging 10 hours each day of your life for a little bit of money. He would never work for an organisation which lacked a soul ever again.

Some would say Mark had 'died' of a broken heart. They would all be wrong. He'd 'died' when the spark went out.

*'If Michelangelo was not ready to redefine what is possible he would have painted 12 frescoes on the Sistine Chapel's floor rather than 300 figures on the ceiling.'*

Anon.

## Chapter 4   The SUSPECT: Me

# Mother of Invention

'Is that your geranium?'

I raise my head and realise that I'm looking into the sun, shaded only by the dark silhouette of a man looking down at me. The sun makes it impossible to see his face but gives him a halo instead.

I'm on all fours trying to read the label of a plant in the 'annuals' section of our local garden centre. Having abandoned my computer and gone into the garden for some sunshine I was almost instantly 'sent out on a mission' to purchase some nasturtiums and geraniums. I'd been told by my other half how upset they all were that I'd been stuffed indoors working on the first fine day of the summer. I'd countered with supreme logic that working during the day was better than working in the evening and would give us more time later in the year. It hadn't worked. Now I'm checking the nasturtiums but I'd left the previously located geraniums in the middle path and had blocked the gentleman's way. 'No problem,' I say chirpily, stretching out my hand to retrieve the offending pots. As I reach across I can now see the face belonging to the cut-out. I recognise it almost immediately. I blurt out, 'It's Franck isn't it?'

'Yes it is,' he replies, extending his arm to shake my outstretched hand. 'And you're going to have to help me.'

'Help you?' I think, 'What with?' It takes me a moment to understand what he means. 'Oh!' I gush suddenly, 'You want to know how I know you?'

He nods in response, a slight smile playing on his lips. He's obviously a bit embarrassed, so I explain how and when we met. Franck nods slowly and sagely as I speak, as if it's all coming back to him. I finish my monologue by explaining what I'm doing at the Garden Centre. I say mournfully, 'Well I made the mistake of running away from a presentation I was putting together and going into our garden – and was promptly "sent out on a mission" here for geraniums and nasturtiums.'

'You were **working** on such a beautiful day?' he asks incredulously, 'and after all the weeks of rain we've had...' his voice tails off.

I'm embarrassed. 'Unfortunately, yes,' I reply.

'It must either be something really important, or something you are really dying to get done,' he suggests helpfully.

'It's just important,' I reply flatly, thinking, 'That makes me seem like a really sad, workaholic nerd.'

'Well, if it was that important I hope you made good progress,' he adds encouragingly.

I snort in disgust at the thought of my wasted time. 'My computer crashed,' I reply, 'and anyway I was getting very stuck. It's to do with my new role as Director of Innovation. I have to update our Executive board tomorrow...' My words stick in my throat.

'And?'

'And it's all not going fast enough,' I say in a strained voice which together with my face betray the fact that I am really stressed and thinking 'I need to get back to work now.'

Franck ignores my obvious glance at my watch. 'Why don't we have a quick cup of tea and you can talk me through it. See if I can offer any ideas or at least act as a sounding board?'

Now we are sitting in the tea rooms. On the traditionally laid round white tablecloth in front of me is spread a scrumptious-looking cream tea. Franck on the other hand has stuck to just tea – and worse, peppermint tea and no scones – the masochist!

'So, tell me,' he asks, **'why does your organisation need all this "innovation" so badly, why does it feel that they need it so much and so structured that they've even appointed someone to direct it?'** and then adds softly, as if to himself, **'isn't it an oxymoron? *Directing innovation...*'**

'Well,' I reply, trying not to be defensive, 'as the world has sped up and business has become global and more complex we've tried to stay on top.'

'Good move,' he responds.

'Initially we did this by trying to maximise our growth. We did this through mergers and acquisitions but the results were disappointing.'

'Why was that?'

**'You see, slapping together two companies to make a bigger one
isn't *real* growth.** It fools the analysts and erases any baselines
for business performance comparisons but at the end of the day
it's just two companies glued together. It's what you do with
them once you have control over both which can, if you're lucky,
lead to growth. But we discovered through the hardship and
heartache of trying to get synergies from opposing cultures,
systems and processes that in reality we were simply taking the
practice of one organisation and forcing it on the other.'

'You couldn't get "best practice"?'

'No, in fact talking about "best practice" seemed to be the best
way to maximise the rifts and resentments between the merged
companies as they battled to demonstrate that their previous
practice was best.'

Franck nods appreciatively.

I continue pouring out my heart to him. 'But the real problem
is, if you think about it, if the two were struggling to grow
when they were smaller and more culturally and strategically
uniform, getting bigger so fast simply brings more pain and
difficulty. Most mergers end up being paid for by the staff with
their salaries.' I pause, smiling grimly. 'And now with what we
euphemistically call the BRIC Wall Challenge (being beaten
on price for a product offering of the same quality) and our
Economic Cliff Challenge (low consumer spending through
debt for some time to come) we've realised that we must stop
playing at this *fake growth by acquisition* game. The real
objective of *that* game was overall global dominance. Our only
real goal should have been dominance – **to get so big that you
can dominate all your stakeholders and then you no longer
need to pay attention to any of your stakeholders, customers,**

**staff, banks, governments or shareholders because you are so dominant.**' I pause for effect to drive my point home.

Frank looks impressed with my logic. 'I guess monopolies have always been a great way to print money,' he retorts.

'The bad news is that *in each market there is only* **one** *dominant company.* We realised that unless a miracle happened we weren't going to win, be the biggest and most **dominant** player in our marketplace in the world. It wasn't going to be us. The other option we had was to try to forge an alliance – a cartel – but that's illegal.'

'So what did you decide to do instead, since you couldn't **Dominate**?' he asks with real curiosity.

'Well, we felt we were left with only two choices – stay on the same track without the dominant scale, jumping from one ineffective strategy to the next, secretly waiting to be snapped up by someone else, thereby allowing the Directors to pocket nice golden parachutes.'

'But that is tantamount to effectively allowing the organisation to **Die**,' he protests.

'Yes, I know,' I reply, 'but you have to admit if you were a director it doesn't seem like that bad an option.'

Franck nods, adding, 'True, it's not a bad option for the directors, but a shame for everyone else. What was your third option?'

'The third option is perhaps the most difficult of the three, and I guess if you're not dominant and if your directors don't want to "sell out" it's really your only choice. We came to the conclusion that **it was necessary to *really* change,** we had to invent a really new way to interact with all our stakeholders, especially the customers and suppliers. We had to **Evolve**, to permanently and sustainably outsmart our competitors. This is going beyond change to what we have called business transformation. Less about fattening the pig, from thin pig to fat pig, more about turning from a caterpillar into a butterfly. So four months ago our CEO announced to the analysts that we were going to become the *"most innovative business in our sector."'*

Franck is nodding and smiling and sipping his peppermint tea. 'Logical,' he says. 'So it's Evolve, Dominate or Die. You can't dominate, you don't want to die so what's the problem?'

I can't hide my exasperation – you can hear it in my voice. 'Everyone seems to want innovation, everyone seems to be – or at least say that they are – supportive of it. They say great things about it but there isn't much of it around. For a start, as a result of all our previous mergers and acquisitions we have very little cash. And all that right-sizing and synergising has left everyone really risk averse. So guess what? Well, nothing's happened. The first guy who was given the role of Director of Innovation quit after a month, citing stress and lack of support from the board and senior management. He said that although they all "rubber-stamped" innovation they didn't really believe in it. I've taken over and now one of our key people, Mark Haddock, who has always been considered as one of our 'young Turks', a real go-getter and very creative, who was leading our best chance at an offer to transform the industry, has just quit too! He was advised by his doctor to see a psychiatrist who told him that he was suffering from UDS.'

'UDS?' asks Frank, his brow undulating in puzzlement.

'Unfulfilled Dream Syndrome,' I reply miserably. 'He's left our highest-profile new product project high and dry and leaderless.'

I pause, filled with frustration and emotion. 'I'm beginning to fear this job is going to be a lot tougher than I thought.' As I say this my voice tightens mid-sentence and rises slightly in volume to match my level of frustration and worry.

------

*'Free advice costs you nothing until you act upon it.'*
Anon.

## Chapter 5   The SUSPECT: The Consultant

# If You Don't Mind, I'll Have Your Watch Please

Gupta Narendrenathan was sending emails. As a Senior Partner of McKlaskeys he liked to keep the Tyros on their toes. 'Tyro' (an out-of-date expression for a student pilot) was how the 'Made Men' (a Mafia expression for the true members of the 'brotherhood' – McKlaskeys' Equal Opportunity Policy did not reflect the mindsets of the key powerbrokers) referred to the cannon fodder they had to keep working flat out at 260 fee-earning days per year until they moved 'up' (to a more senior position) or 'out' (left behind in a client organisation like a cold war 'sleeper' ready to be awakened so the next time McKlaskeys wanted to milk the client they would have a person on the inside).

Gupta loved sending out these Sunday emails. He knew the electrifying effect it had on the Tyros who would arrive at work only to discover that they were already behind and would need to shift immediately into the highest gear just to stand still – productivity at its best. The market was hot – the firm's multi-million investment in marketing their ability to help clients deliver innovation was paying off handsomely and there was a need to see how much they could take out of it now. Speed was important. But sometimes there were little hiccups. The project they had started at ALCORP showed lots of promise for providing a return on all that marketing investment. It had at its centre a CEO who had publicly 'nailed his colours' to the *innovation* mast – this effectively condemned him to spend, spend and spend until he could point at enough 'innovation' to justify his promises. Great news for McKlaskeys. Except for the fact that simultaneously engaging McKlaskeys he had appointed a Director of Innovation. Now how does that work? Either he wants McKlaskeys to drive it or he wants the Director of Innovation to drive it. If he trusted the Director of Innovation to deliver he'd have let *him* select, appoint and brief the consultants. Gupta smiled to himself slyly – McKlaskeys was safe. And the 2000 fee-earning days were safe, provided the new director's credibility could be kept down long enough whilst savaging the credibility of any internal competition and intrapreneurs. Gupta leaned back in his chair. He knew why he always suggested that a new client undertake a 'benchmarking'. They always agreed and they always came out badly. It was money for old rope. Of course they would come out badly. If they'd been brilliant at innovation they wouldn't have engaged McKlaskeys. The best part of the benchmarking output was the way, as a by-product, it discredited any internal entrepreneurs. So far so good at ALCORP. The report benchmarking their innovations in the pipeline had savaged several of them quite satisfactorily.

---

*'Creativity is to Innovation what Beef is to Tournedos Rossini:*
*just a starting point.'*
Christophe Gillet

## Chapter 6   The SUSPECT: Me

# I Wouldn't Have Started From Here

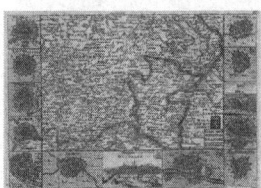 'Take me through this again; you say **your organisation needs desperately to deliver more with less? And innovation is the route?**'

I nod in response to each question. 'And we need to become far more creative,' I reply.

'And yet somehow **the people in your organisation are not moving fast enough to re-imagine what they do, how they do it and who they do it with or for?**'

I nod enthusiastically. It's not exactly how I would have put it but it's close enough. 'I know it sounds as if our people are unaware of the challenge of becoming more creative. I mean it's not as if they haven't been told.'

'What do you mean, "Told"?' he asks, brow furrowed.

'Well, after our CEO announced his intentions to the analysts he made a company-wide announcement telling people clearly what was expected of them.'

Franck grins broadly and unexpectedly, leans back in his chair and almost guffaws as he says, 'You mean he told them he expected them to be creative?'

'Yes,' I reply slowly, confused at his reaction, 'and stated the goal of being the sector leader. He said that he was *encouraging them to take risks*. He said that he expected people to fail. He also announced that consultants would be helping us to establish an innovation process.' I finish firmly.

Franck's smile has subsided. He looks subdued if slightly sick. 'Will you allow me to gaze into my crystal ball and tell you what I think has happened since?' he offers.

'Yeah. Sure,' I reply, perplexed. What a strange offer. How can he possibly know what has happened in our organisation? He's never even visited us and nothing's been published in the news.

He begins. 'For a start, the level of cynicism of staff, especially middle ranking staff in your organisation has risen immensely. Most people are finding all sorts of reasons why it is not possible to come up with anything new. The only ideas which are coming through are people's favourite old ones which have been out in the daylight and shelved several times before. In fact, they often present what has been standard practice for years in one or other of your pre-merger organisations as if it's a "great new idea".'

He is watching me closely as he speaks, searching my face for a reaction to see if his guesses are correct. I'm giving nothing away.

'The only "newish" ideas are coming from people who are relatively new to the organisation and are effectively versions of normal practice in their previous jobs, and anyway they don't fit customer needs, the stated business strategy or the capability of your organisation to execute them. The few ideas which have made it through your new, "consultant-inspired" innovation process are finding it difficult to justify even the investment you have made in them so far, let alone more.'

By now I'm finding it difficult to remain poker-faced.

'All the people you had been hoping would help to lead the implementation of the new innovation process are suddenly very busy with client management and revenue generation activities. To top it all, no one is sticking their neck out at all. In fact, the level of "cover your anatomy" e-mails that are circulating around the organisation is severely challenging the bandwidth of your intranet connections. Everyone is right behind the initiative but far enough behind to have lost touch.'

I've lost the game of poker. My face shows it. My jaw is slack, my forehead slightly shiny from perspiration and I look stunned. Each statement he made felt like being smacked in the mouth. I feel the pain of the past months sharply. He's absolutely right. Every single statement describes what's happened in the past few months. But how does he know? How does he know all this has happened to me? I haven't said anything about what's happened. And if it's all so obvious to him **why didn't we know that it was going to happen?** I can't find any words.

Franck's observing me closely like a hawk about to pounce on a poor unprotected rabbit. He is taking in my expressions and reaction to his words.

'How do you know all this?' I ask. 'Do you know someone else in our company?'

He smiles warmly. 'No I don't. The reason I can predict what is happening to you is because I've seen the same pattern elsewhere in other organisations. You see, I've been trying to understand **the paradox of innovation for some time. With the level of change and global competition, every business enterprise and corporation wants it. With many governments insolvent and an urgent need to deliver services to their citizens without spending money, many Governments want it. With the super-wealthy unable to find anything to buy or invest in at their scale except more assets which generate value but no real wealth. Everybody seems to want it. Everybody seems to need it. Everyone seems to have a process for it. Over seventy thousand books have been written about it. And yet there is so little of it about!'**

I can't think of a suitable reply.

Franck waits patiently for a moment for me to respond. Eventually he says, 'From the look on your face, I would guess you need another cup of tea or something stronger, but I think it's going to have to be tea,' and without my confirmation he waves energetically at the waitress.

---

*'A good solution can be successfully applied to almost any problem.'*
Ed Murphy

## Chapter 7   The SUSPECT: The Chief Financial Officer

# Weeding Out the Weaklings

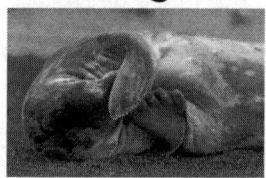 Burt Knox knew it would be a waste of time, and it is. In his experience, about every ten years, like an unpleasant prize in a pass-the-parcel game, it came round again. Once again 'innovation' was in vogue. He's seen it before. Millions would be wasted in 'exciting breakthrough projects' which were supposed to lift the company's fortunes, and yet... And yet, they always managed to fail to meet a fraction of the volume of expectations and promises they had made and had to be canned. Often with the loss of several hundred staff to pay for the waste. And then we went back to normal. Back to the normal hard grind of making money without any fancy ideas.

He would do his best to stop the waste. He would insist on business cases, market data and good numbers. You didn't know where you were unless you had the numbers. They would 'namby-pamby' around saying things like, 'It's new so we can't estimate the market.' or 'Everyone will want this,' or tell him stories from academic MBA case studies of how such and such a company had put a business case together for something like social networking and underestimated by a factor of a million. But from his point of view he was firm. No sound business case, no investment!

Slowly, as he ruminated, his plan formed. He would attend all the key meetings, listening and nodding, leaning back in his well worn chair in the executive boardroom, and let the presentation from the new, wet-behind-the-ears Director of Innovation wash over him.

Burt had learnt long ago, even before he qualified as an accountant, how to listen with a questioning and sceptical but unchanging expression on his face.

Burt had been CFO six times in two companies – that was the joy of merging and restructuring. He knew the pattern.

He knew how the investment community worked – three groups of baying hounds.

On the one hand the sellers who really didn't care if people bought or sold as long as they bought or sold at volume – they didn't really care if the shares which passed through their hands were destined to be real investment funds for driving real growth or if it was just the normal speculation and gambling which represented 80% of the trades they managed.

In the other corner were the media – the juicier and more lurid the gossip and crises the better. They needed eyeballs. Eyeballs meant sales and sales meant more advertising revenue and subscription.

The final pack of hounds, the institutional investors – for them 'more was better' – all they cared about was the funds under their control – the bigger the funds under management the bigger the slice of the pie they could greedily cut for themselves.

And finally there was his company battling to ensure the lowest cost of capital and enough free cash to ensure that they actually could operate profitably.

To play the game you had to have a good story – he smiled wryly to himself – or fairy tale – and this was where the problem arose – a real confusion between the story which promised growth through innovation and the reality of innovation. He'd never seen growth through innovation for real. Yes, he'd seen businesses buy start-ups, alliances and gain control over breakthrough technology but never, never ever 'real innovation' in a corporate. 'Real innovation', as in 'a barmy idea turning into billions'. Most innovation he had concluded was an attempt to 'squeeze sunlight out of flowers'. To try to innovate systematically he believed was like asking advice from a lottery winner on how to win the lottery.

**Burt knew that the most responsible thing he could do was to do what he always did which was to make sure he had control over the funding of projects, kill off the crazy ones and limit spending as much as possible.**

He'd remembered reading that even mighty corporate software giants, who were supposed to be really innovative, once they'd made it with a core product had then gone on to buy almost everything they had branded – from email packages to instant messaging to image manipulation software. Why should his company do things differently? Let someone else lose his shirt and break his back inventing something new. Once it was proven, as long as we could cheaply reach into deep pockets, we could buy them up. It made far more sense than this 'let's be innovative' fad. But Burt was smart enough to never say so. So at the end of the one-hour-long presentation by the Director of Innovation he would suggest, apparently helpfully, 'You know, you've got some really good opportunities coming up – what we need to ensure is that the best, lowest-risk ideas aren't starved of capital. I need you to make sure we have a good assessment panel so that we can ensure that we really move the agenda forward. As chairman of the pipeline assessment panel I'd like us to spend some further time together to "weed out the weaklings" and build on the strongest opportunities.' He knew that this was his takeover bid. With this move he would control this innovation 'fad.' The stupid, crazy, impractical ideas would be eliminated. Capital spend would be linked to stage-gates and business cases, and no money would be wasted. He knew as CFO that people always forgot **that it was much, much easier to *spend* money which you had than to *earn* revenues which you didn't have.**

He knew that he would soon be in control and could put an end to all this nonsense. He would make the Director of Innovation an offer which 'wouldn't be refused'. In his experience it never had been.

———————————

*'Nothing works by itself, just to please you. You've got to <u>make</u> the damn thing work!'*

T. Edison

## Chapter 8   The SUSPECT: Me

## Still Hunting and Gathering

'So, honestly,' I say quizzically, 'how *do* you know what has been happening to me?'

'Easy,' he replies. 'You violated New World Rules[2] several times. Also ignored the First Instruction for Innovation,' he pauses briefly in reflection, 'and especially the Third Law of Change[3] over and over.' He adds absentmindedly, 'the Fifth Law of Change – once...' His voice trails off as if he's thinking about something other than what he's saying. And then he seems to switch energetically back into our conversation. **'To me this means that you will stay in the pretty predictable but unpleasant "old world" pattern,'** he finishes forcefully.

'Laws? Third Law of Change?' I repeat, trying to make some sense of what he is saying. 'What Laws? Innovation has Instructions? Now who's the oxymoron?' I say, confused but amused at my wit.

'Sure,' he replies coolly, 'Just like in physics. Our new world has distinct rules you need to follow if you want to survive

---

2   From *New Rules for the New World*. Eddie Obeng.
3   From *All Change!* Eddie Obeng.

and thrive in it rather than become a victim. Innovation has Instructions and Change has real Laws. Transformation has Slogans. For example, "**People create change – People constrain change.**" That's the Third Law of Change. *"If it's not hurting it's not working,"* is a popular Transformation slogan.' He quickly adds, 'The slogans, unlike the Instructions of Innovation or Law of Change, aren't scientifically based.'

I don't get it and it's obvious in the expression on my face.

Franck's hands are animated. From the way they are oscillating to and fro you can tell that he is trying hard to find a simple way to explain a complex idea to 'old thicko' here. And then he starts to speak animatedly. 'Have you noticed how your own ideas are brilliant and other people's are not quite so?'

I smile at the thought.

'Did you ever go to a meeting with your new idea, show it off only to have everyone beat it with a stick? In fact, the only person who sides with you says something like, "I think this has some merit. In fact I had a similar idea myself only yesterday"...'

I nod. I recognise the scenario. It's happened to me a lot.

'Quite simply,' he explains patiently, 'human beings aren't really designed for too much change. Well, they sort of are and sort of aren't. If you surprise them with something new, all that *fight or flight* stuff kicks in,[4] their logic circuits get turned off. Do you know why?'

Sure I know about fight or flight but what does that have to do with thinking logically? I ponder a second and reply, 'I guess

---

4   From *The Complete Leader*. Eddie Obeng.

in times of danger, thinking is too slow. You need to act on instinct.'

'Precisely!' he replies. 'And that is why when someone says something which surprises you in a meeting you often can't come up with the right response immediately. **Your logic circuits are switched off by the question. The "surprise question" also triggers your emotions, usually fear, and pumps you full of adrenaline** which is why, in the meeting, your palms start to sweat and your stomach fills with hyperactive butterflies. Hours later, perhaps in the evening, it suddenly comes to you with a jolt. "What I should have said to him was…" It only comes to you once the adrenaline has drained away and the immediate emotion subsided.'

'So?' I challenge, shrugging my shoulders and shaking my head rapidly from side to side.

Franck ignores my question and just asks another. 'Did you ever try to get a logical response from someone in an emotional state?'

I think only briefly about the short conversation I'd had with my other half before I'd been banished to the garden centre. 'It doesn't work.'

'Correct,' he agrees, clipping the word and adding an upward inflexion. 'When you are surprised, your logic switches off, your emotions switch on and you take your stance emotionally. And can you beat an emotional stance with logic?'

I wince as I remember the conversation I'd had with my other half earlier in the day. I'd tried to logically argue my way through, only making matters worse. The word 'No' escapes squeakily from my lips.

'And you therefore meet incoming logical ideas with solid emotional resistance. You then justify your rejection of these logical ideas with smokescreen arguments to hide the fact that there is no logical reason for the rejection.'

I nod, trying to follow his argument.

'On the other hand, **when *you* have an idea**, well that's your "baby". **You literally fall in love with your own ideas**. Often you'll fight tooth and nail to make it happen. Well that's the *Third Law of Change*. **People create change – People constrain change.**'

'Oh!' I exclaim, at a loss at what else to say. Then my natural scepticism kicks in. 'That can't be right, or we'd never accept anyone else's ideas. Why, only last week I presented an idea for improving ideas collection to my team and after discussion one of them agreed it was a brilliant idea and that they would like to work with me on it.'

Franck pauses briefly, a wicked smile playing on his lips. 'What exactly was the offer? Was it, *"That's a brilliant idea. I've never heard anything like it before. I want to work on it"*? Or was it *"This is a brilliant idea. It reminds me of something I've been thinking about for a while. I want to work on it"*?'

'The second one,' I reply tentatively.

Franck's guffaw is loud and annoying. 'Or in other words *"The idea you have just told me looks a lot like my own idea. I would be happy to use your resources to work on my own idea"*?'

I feel crushed. I'd never thought about it that way. It's not my idea they're supporting after all – it's their own. I'm starting to feel emotional about this conversation but Franck gives me no time to boil.

'Now think about it, your CEO announced the "innovation focus". That's a bit like jumping out from behind a bush and shouting YAH! at a caveman. What sort of response would that get?'

I shrug my shoulders. 'I guess they'd either run away or throw a spear at you.'

Franck laughs out loud, his head bobbing about rapidly. 'But what was worse was that the message was even more frightening than YAH! because it was from the boss. And the boss was not even telling you HOW to make it OK. An instruction from someone more powerful in the organisation than you asking you to do something you imagine is impossible and then not giving guidance is just like someone much bigger and stronger than you,' he rises out of his chair to tower over me like a bird of prey with wings outstretched, 'instructing you to, "Be spontaneous."' He pauses, then for effect, screams the word, 'Now!'

I'm nodding silently and rhythmically as I get the message.

'So, having frightened them and got them into a real emotionally resistant state, he then tells them to "take risks"!'

'What's wrong,' I challenge, 'with asking people to take risks?'

Franck repeats what I've said as if completely astounded by my question, '"What's wrong with asking people to take risks?" Your CEO says *"Take risks"* – but what the colleagues hear is totally different. Remember, all their logic circuits have been turned off by the YAH! and are still off. As the words *"Take risks"* leave the mouth of the CEO, who up till now has fired people for missing targets and making mistakes, the words are miraculously transformed so instead of *"Take risks"* what they actually hear is, *"This business is in such real trouble that I, your CEO, don't know what to do, so all our jobs are on the line. I want you to throw yourself upon your sword. Wipe out years of getting your colleagues to respect and trust you and instead do some stupid rash things. Oh yes, and be sure to fail often!"* They know that failing is not a smart thing to do and also if the organisation is in such trouble, when the time comes to chop heads the first to go will be the losers who took risks and failed! You must understand – we live in an increasingly risk-averse world, a world of firewalls, health & safety, "lessons learned", class-action lawsuits. To take risks is almost seen as immoral. So you took risks, now you've been fired. Go back home and tell your other half and your hungry children what you did!'

My mouth has gone completely dry and my face feels hot. Described that way it's the most stupid speech possible. It's not surprising we received the reception we got. I don't have the courage to tell Franck that I wrote the speech. I blurt out, 'But you've got to take risks if you want to innovate.' I am repeating what our consultants have told me.

'No!' barks Franck, adding more gently, 'Actually you don't. **In innovation the last thing you want to do is to take risks**. It's so difficult to succeed, that what you need to do is to *avoid taking risks*. That's why it's fashionable to *start the process with customer insights*. That way you can be sure that they, someone, will want your innovation.'

I remember my thoughts earlier today when my computer crashed, but that was just an emotional response to techno-failure – but this, this was innovation, this was different. 'No risks?' I say with incredulity. I've read tons of books on innovation and taking risks is one thing that they are very keen on. 'But surely…' I recite the phrase, 'Speculate to accumulate?'

'A good slogan can prevent analysis for fifty years,' Franck ripostes sharply. 'I mean it. **No, no risks!**' he repeats adding, '**And the goal isn't to be more creative**.' He smiles as he drops another bombshell on my confidence.

I'm unconvinced. As I start to question him he notices the time on the clock on the wall and leaps up exclaiming, 'Oh my goodness, I'm really late.'

He fishes in his jacket pocket for something, something small which he fails to find. 'I thought I had a calling card. Never mind, QUBE me and we can continue our conversation.'

'Cube you?' I ask, completely confused.

'Yes,' he says, 'QUBE me… on PC or Mac… look on the internet. I know I can meet you at 1:15 on Tuesday for about 40 minutes.'

'What? Where? I have to be out of the country Tuesday.'

'No problem, that's why I said "QUBE me" around lunch-time if you are taking a break. And,' he adds mysteriously, 'remember, *for your innovations to succeed, you will have to discover who or what is killing the sparks*.' With that he shakes my hand firmly and is gone.

---

## Chapter 9   The SUSPECT: The Chief Operating Officer

## It May Be Effective but Is It Efficient?

 It's hard enough being Head of Operations in a world where customers are never satisfied, call centres are never fast enough and the only way you can get things delivered to the right cost is through a 5000-mile-long supply chain! It was 5:52 a.m. and Zhang Min had just sprinted the last two flights of stairs up to her office rather than wait for the geriatric lift. As usual for a Monday morning she had a conference call due with their outsource partners on the other side of the world. Breakfast for her, dinner for them. It had to be done. She patiently waited the three free minutes she got every morning as her laptop booted up. She'd already worked out that three minutes a day over a working year was ten hours. Ten hours! That was longer than the legislated European working day! Perhaps she should get a tablet… but all that swooshing, sweeping and swiping… it wasn't natural, so she'd learnt how to use the time for meditation. She had even taught herself how to type in her password 'on autopilot' and answer all the various pointless questions the machine asked her each morning. Questions to which the answers were the same as the previous morning and yet the machine never learned.

She was upbeat today. Last week there had been a dark cloud on the horizon. The prospect of a major new product offer. The disruption to existing operations would have been terrible.

Not to mention the impact on security testing and customer response times and call centre training. It wasn't that she was against new things – she wasn't. It's just that sometimes when you've been working hard to get smooth operation, novelty is just a disruption. In truth Min was actually feeling a little guilty. Her report on the cannibalisation of the existing products and the operational impact costs of the new offer had not been positive. She felt in some way guilty for the cancellation of the project and the resignation of Mark. Mark after all was a good guy – energetic, keen and genuinely determined to help the business. But some things just couldn't be helped and this was one of them.

---

*'The beaten path is safest but the traffic is terrible.'*
Jeff Taylor

## Chapter 10   The SUSPECT: Me

# Ha. You Failed!

I'd survived the meeting. Fortunately, as always, the ExCo were running late so the length of my presentation had been cut from an hour to 20 minutes. There had been a lot of concern about the loss of Mark and the failure of the most promising innovation in the pipeline. John Troy our CEO had asked me to 'make a "full presentation" of an hour and a half next Friday' to explain what had happened and to make sure it wasn't repeated. His actual words were, 'We must make sure that this failure thing doesn't become a habit. Once is enough.'

I'd managed to convince them that we were making good progress. I'd updated them with the figures from our ideas management software demonstrating how many more ideas we were adding to the top of our funnel model. They seemed impressed. The CFO seemed particularly concerned about the effectiveness of our stage-gate process and asked me about it twice. He wanted to be certain that unpromising projects would be terminated without waste of resources. He'd said that to demonstrate his support he'd be happy to sit on the Innovation Review Panel. I felt pleased that he'd offered. I must have done a good job with my presentation. He rarely ever offers to contribute. His style is more of a 'tell me' and 'give me numbers' poker-faced approach.

The Marketing Director seemed keen to know how new initiatives would be incorporated in the current portfolio of offers. I didn't have an answer but responded non-committally, suggesting that his advice would be welcome. This seemed to satisfy him. Although, unlike Burt Knox, he hadn't offered to get his hands dirty. Our CEO summed up my presentation saying, 'The sooner we develop a risk-taking culture in this organisation the better. We need to make sure people are comfortable with failure. It's OK to fail but don't fail twice.' I listen to his concluding remarks and then realise that my mouth has dropped open. I don't have the time or courage to share with him what I learnt from Franck.

At my afternoon update with our consultants I'd mentioned Franck's comments about not surprising our people with our challenging announcements on creativity and, even more strangely, his comments on not taking risks.

The lead consultant had placed his hands in his lap in the temple position and replied, 'We have very extensive experience of leveraging innovation in an organisation and I can assure you that the way we are approaching it is how it's done. I've never heard of or read of any of the quaint ideas your friend mentioned.' I leave the update meeting perplexed.

So I've searched the internet for 'cube'. Everything from bicycles to shapes to shoes but no sign of Franck, so I try again typing in 'Franck cube'. Jackpot! The search engine offers me http:// QUBE.cc. I click, download the app and now I seem to be loading something. My screen turns grey momentarily and then a greyed out picture of a room holds whilst the message 'Loading Office' explains the lengthening green bar which grows horizontally across the screen. A moment, a ping and I'm in. I'm also confused. I'm staring across a room with a shiny wooden floor, out of a window which seems to look out over parked cars. To the left of the screen is a huge whiteboard next to a bookcase.

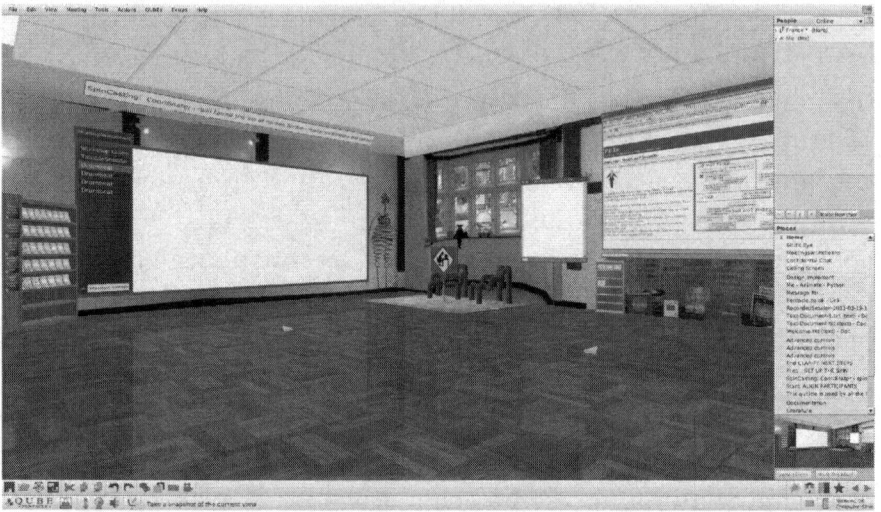

'Your mic is off. Turn it on.' It's Franck's voice.

I reply, 'How do I...'

'Look at the menu icons in the bottom toolbar,' comes the answer. As I click on the microphone icon turning it from red to green, a strange, green, boxy figure, some sort of plank-like avatar, appears in the middle of my view. Hovering inches above its square head there is a plaque which reads 'Franck'. The facial features of the head are minimalist. A smiley with twinkling eyes as if drawn on the green background with charcoal. Suddenly the face disappears. Then, like an old fashioned TV set coming on, it turns into a grey square for a fraction of a second and then the head of the avatar displays Franck's real face. Smiling. It takes me a second to realise that this must be off the webcam at his end.

'Er, hello,' I stutter.

'Great. Let's get to it and work out what you want from this conversation.' His avatar swings round and heads for the bookcase, a green laser flashes from the avatar and seems to pick up and drag an item from the bookcase onto the whiteboard. I watch, transfixed. A large poster unfolds on the whiteboard. Written vertically up the side are the words 'Hopes&Fears™'.

'Come on,' he says, 'come closer and let's work out what you want from this conversation and what you'd like us to avoid.'

I lean towards my computer screen.

'Come on, come closer,' he says, barely hiding his impatience.

'How do I…?'

'Like a computer game,' he replies. 'W or S to go back and forward A and D to turn, or you can use the arrow keys. The rest is intuitive. Your mouse is your hand. Use it to point and move things and right-click to get a menu of what the object can do for you. Right?'

'Right. OK,' I reply, pressing a button and skidding off in the opposite direction from the one I wanted.

Now I've settled in. On the whiteboard in front of us there is an array of sticky notes proclaiming my hopes and fears. My hopes include *'finding out why our consultants disagree with Franck'* and *'how to speed up innovation in our organisation'*. My sole fear is *'running out of time'*.

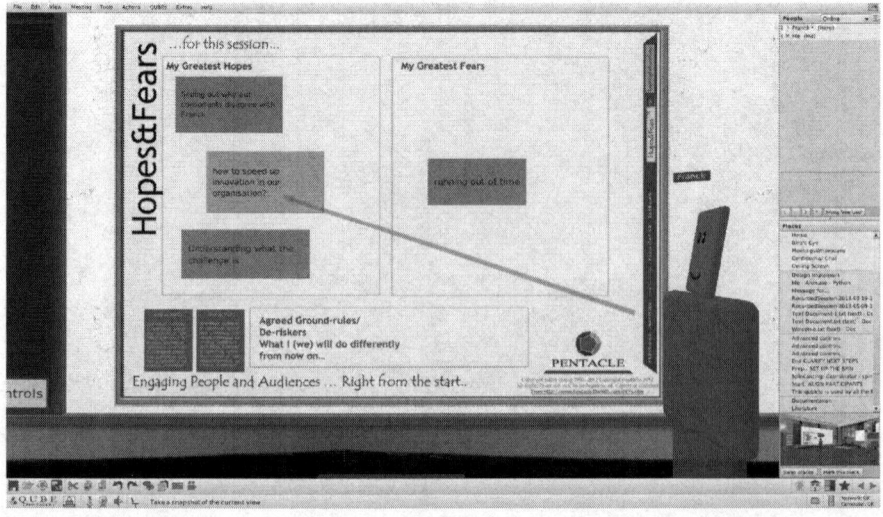

Franck drags the sticky notes up and down the poster arranging the hopes, top-to-bottom, in a timeline to give us an instant agenda. I think to myself, 'that's a neat trick'.

'I've shared your comments about not taking risks at work and it seems that everyone disagrees with you. They say that everybody knows that it is not only essential to give permission to people to be creative, it is also critical to take risks.'

Franck chuckles. 'You say everybody knows?'

'Yes,' I reply confidently.

'Let's sit down,' he says, clicking on a chair at the table in the middle of the virtual room (which I have just learnt is called a qubicle).

I click on an adjacent chair and am now facing his qubot (which, I have just learnt, is what the boxy avatars are called on QUBE).

'Well, if everybody knows then I must be mistaken – maybe the world <u>is</u> flat after all. If popularity was truth we'd all want to eat what flies love to eat. There are far more of them than there are of us,' he says wickedly, adding, as if he is quoting someone else, '"*Of course not being known doesn't stop the truth being true!*"'[5]

I ignore his third sentence and ponder the self-evident truth of his second sentence whilst reacting to the arrogance of the first.

He continues. 'Imagine we were standing at the edge of a cliff and I said "jump off but don't worry, there is no risk because you are attached to a stout, strong line and you have a parachute packed in your backpack." Or imagine that I said that it was good to take risks so I'd attached you to the line with a piece of string which *may or may not break*. With a parachute *which may or may not open*. Which scenario do you think would induce you to jump?'

I can see his point but I can't agree. 'But surely he must be wrong. All the books, our CEO, the consultants were adamant about risk taking.' I open my mouth but no sound comes out. Instead I move my mouse back and forth, nodding the head of my virtual qubot – me.

He says, again as if quoting someone else, '"*Everyone thinks that people who do unsafe, dangerous things are daredevils, risk-takers, but they are wrong. People who do unsafe things have to be very safe indeed if they are to survive!*"'

I open my mouth again but still no sound comes out.

'You see, people confuse taking risks with failure. Remember you were telling me about the time before the crisis, crunch,

5   Richard Bach.

BRIC Challenge and austerity measures, in the early days of globalisation, how it was possible to build upon organisational experience?'

'Yep,' I reply.

'Hmm, well it probably wasn't. You see, about fifteen years ago...' he begins seriously, 'at midnight...'

I laugh.

'... For many of us the combined pace, scope and scale, and interactivity of the world outstripped our ability to learn. This was mostly because there were more of us on the planet better connected at the speed of cyberspace and many interested in moving from their status quo. From that point onwards it was difficult to see the reality of what was going on versus what we believed should be going on. Individuals thought they were getting richer whilst many were just piling up debt. Governments, advised by their economists, confused an increase in value with an increase in wealth and bankrupted themselves. Individuals who did save found their savings transported round the globe to be used to buy the goods and services they themselves were producing at very low rates. For many of us it was a huge party. Record profits, record bonuses, record takeovers one after the next after the next. It was obviously completely broken, but because people felt good and thought they were getting rich no one questioned the reality.'

I recognise the scenario he is painting even if I don't agree with everything he says.

🎥 'There's a great video... here,' 🎥 he points to the bottom shelf of the bookcase. It's about ten minutes long. Come back into this qubicle and watch it if you get the chance. Anyway,' – he begins to draw on the main screen. 'So when the pace of the world outstripped the pace of learning… that was midnight.'

I can't see what this has to do with anything so I say, 'I can't see what this has to do with anything.'

'Just assume that I'm approximately right for a while, at least until you've watched the video.'

I nod reluctantly again, both me and my qubot, and say, 'OK.'

'Well, that's where a lot of our misconceptions about risk and failure arise. In that "old world before midnight" we only had one type of failure. Because **the assumption was that for everything you did there was experience somewhere in the company or with a specialist.** So if you got it wrong and failed, it was *your* fault. In such a case how should you be treated?'

'I guess if you got wrong something you could have got right by being a bit more professional and focused or taking advice, you should be treated harshly with no mercy!' As I answer I know this is the 'wrong' answer. Why, only earlier today our CEO had said failure was OK. It is both politically correct and fashionable to talk about 'learning' and 'allowing people the space to fail'. I retract my statement. 'Perhaps they need training to be more professional,' I say, but I think 'Why is it unacceptable to treat the *wasters* as harshly as possible?'

Franck guesses that I'm perplexed. 'The conundrum you see in **the "new world", where the business and organisational environment changes faster than we can learn, is that there is another of type of failure.** Another flavour if you like.'

'What do you mean?' I splutter, confused.

'Imagine,' he says confidentially, 'that instead of doing something other people around you might have experience of – instead – **what you are attempting is completely different.** Never been done in your context before. No matter how much advice you take no one has quite seen this before. However, you attempt to seize the opportunity. You do everything you can to involve key stakeholders who might contribute to the success. Brainstorm in advance all the things which could go wrong and resolve them as early as possible. A friend of mine coined a word for this mindset – **prelimination.**[6] And yet you fail. Fail badly, embarrassingly and publicly. Badly. How should you be treated this time?'

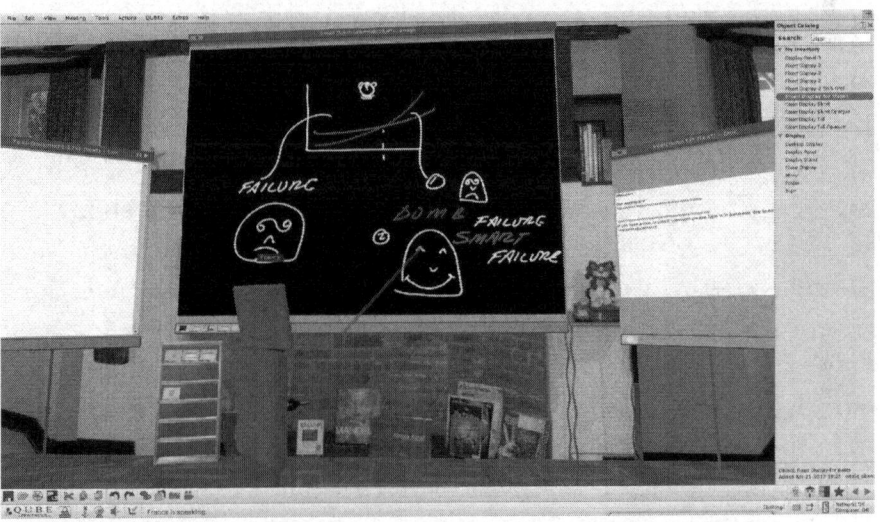

I snort as the realisation dawns and suggest tentatively, 'Congratulated on trying? On getting on with it and not hanging about waiting?'

---

6    This word was suggested to me by David Guy who came up to me after a conference presentation. I think it's brilliant.

'Yes!' he agrees enthusiastically, 'Praised in public for trying. Asked to write-up and share what you've learnt and given a lifetime's supply of free beer and pizzas as a reward.'

I laugh.

🎥 'The first scenario is called **dumb failure** or stupid failure because it could have been prevented. The second is called **smart failure** or intelligent failure because it couldn't. They are very different situations. Before you can judge failure you need to know which scenario it is. Do you think it would be far more useful in your organisation to talk about **encouraging smart failure and of course discouraging dumb failure** and to stop talking that blathering nonsense about risk?' 🎥

He is making me feel a bit stupid but I get his point.

But Franck isn't finished with me yet. 'You see, it's not about risk-taking – it's about doing something outside your norm. Doing something outside the norm may feel uncomfortable but it is not necessarily risky!'

The penny has finished dropping. **All that talk of risk is actually macho nonsense.** I suspect it has a severe negative impact on our ability to innovate. It distracts us from what is really important – **gaining the courage and focus to try things outside our norm.** Putting energy in to make sure that we are being as safe as possible by exploring all the things which otherwise might go wrong and eliminating them before they do. Franck is right. **Innovation has nothing to do with *taking* risks.** I'm enjoying the feeling of this breakthrough, savouring the moment of understanding when I notice Franck is still talking.

'I guess if your organisation is so wedded to risk-taking you must also have some sort of "pipeline" process,' he states boldly.

I nod, trying to figure out how he knows this. I'm sure I haven't mentioned our process and say 'Uhuh.'

'Oh dear! Is that the time?' he exclaims

I look up at the circular wooden clock in the qubicle. It shows my local time. I have no idea what his local time is.

'Look, before I apparate could you do some homework before next time? There you go.' he says dropping a document on my slate. 'Please could you complete this HealthCheck?'

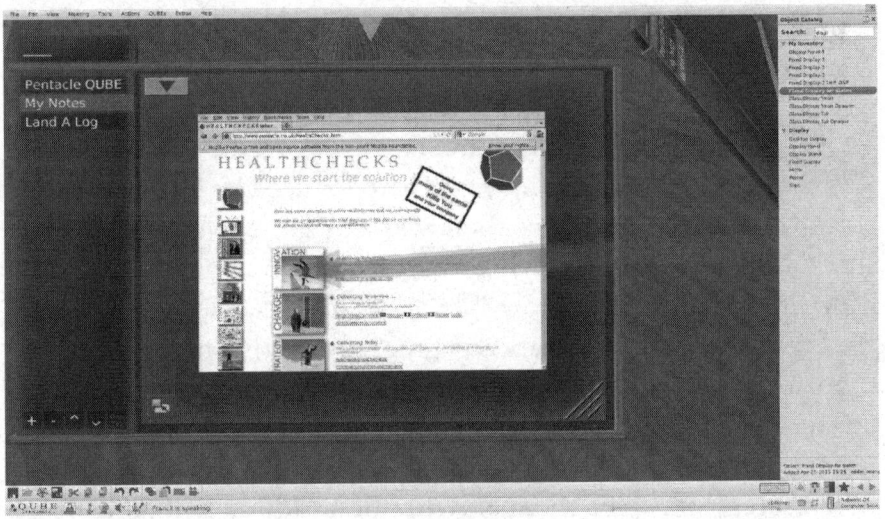

'Sure,' I say hurriedly

'See you soon. Bye,' and he's gone.

---

*Apparently, when* New Scientist *wanted to propose and publish a word for 'making-things-worse-whilst-trying-to-improve-them', they came up with 'Schlimmbesserung.'*
*The real German word is 'Verschlimmbesserung.'*
*So 'Schlimmbesserung' was a 'Verschlimmbesserung'!*

## Chapter 11   The SUSPECT: The Customer

## Damnit! They've Only Gone and *Improved* It!

Al King is shaking his head slowly from side to side. Now he rubs his eyes. It's the sense of betrayal which gets to him. He's known John Troy for years, been loyal and bought from them for decades and now they go and do this to him. Once there was a purpose to buying from them. It made him special. It gave him an advantage. It made him different. But now. Now. Now they have decided to 'extend the brand range to new market segments'. All this means is that there is no advantage to him buying from them. It's great for the new customers. They. They get access to stuff that they would never have dreamed of but, for him… What's the advantage? Their new strategy may give them growth but it is disadvantaging him. Betrayal… after all these years. He says out loud, 'It's as if they've taken the profits they've made from me and decided to give the world a hand up to take away my advantage.' He rubs his left eye slowly with his left hand. The world seems to have stopped thinking. They're all following the same strategy, from the same book, without thinking where it will get them. It's just the same as two decades ago when businesses outsourced and fired staff who had been loyal to them all their lives as part of a get-rich strategy. But everyone did the same, so in the end there was no real advantage to outsourcing. Just a huge disadvantage of lost knowledge and expertise and a new workforce who wouldn't trust them or be loyal but who, now, like mercenaries, will shift and jump to the highest bidder. Thank goodness for the recession. At least that slowed down the churn. He smiles inwardly to himself and then… And then he remembers the 'Introductory Offer' and his eyes burn with tears of rage. So now they are also punishing him for his loyalty. *He* doesn't get any money off. Only the people they are introducing as competition for him. So they are in effect subsidising others to compete with him! He says out loud, 'I'm a fool not to move on. But who would I switch to? They're all just as bad as each other. I'd have to set up my purchasing department differently to constantly be on the lookout for where to jump to next.' Then a thin smile stretches his lips as he thinks wryly, 'at least I'd get the Introductory Discount.'

He sits at a desk and starts to scan the emails. He pauses. 'New Version?' His palms begin to sweat and the rhythm of his breathing quickens. He's been here before. Of course all his team want the latest, the newest. They want to be trained in using it. It's great for them – exciting and it refreshes their CVs, making it easier to jump, but what is the business case for him, for this enterprise?

Take that recent software upgrade. His CIO had insisted that since the platform they were on was no longer 'supported' they needed to upgrade. In his simple mind Al couldn't understand this. The longer a piece of software had been around the more stable it became and there were fewer new bugs to find. He really didn't get it. Most people used a small fraction of what each piece of software was capable of. Surely to upgrade should mean to more fully use what you already had? But No! 'Everyone knows that we must *progress* and *progress* means *upgrades* and *upgrades* mean doing something *different* – we assume that doing *different* is the same as doing *better*'. That now familiar thin smile stretches across his face again… And also you incorporated a stable piece of software into your organisation and based your strategic and operational decisions on it. He raised his eyes from the screen. The way their email platform was configured allowed him and all the members of the ELT to see all of each other's key correspondence without all that 'have I copied you in?', 'please send it again' nonsense. It made perfect sense. After all they were a team. Teams were interdependent and didn't keep secrets from each other. Teams shared a goal and went out of their way to help each other so if the other members of the team knew what you were working on they could help without having to ask. And they were definitely what the title suggested, an Extended Leadership Team. Their email software underpinned people's behaviours and habits. Because everyone on a project could see everyone else on the project or client accounts correspondence the culture was forced open. It was almost impossible to play organisational politics using cc and blind cc and embarrassing for you if you tried to use email tags to cover-your-anatomy. 'We have the culture right and the email software underpins the behaviours and mindsets we want'. Upgrades could break useful working patterns and scatter tacit knowledge. In all his career he had never been able to make a business case for an upgrade stand up. For this new upgrade it would mean the costs of the upgrade, replacement of equipment, probably leading to further upgrades because the new computers would probably have been 'improved'. Then there was the training time and cost and the practising or learning-on-the-job time and the inefficiency everyone will have to suffer – the lost work. He's guessing across the business and over the course of a year the costs will run into the tens of thousands. 'I wonder what we will get in return? On the hard side maybe some processes will go slightly faster. We may be able to retire one or two of our systems. On the soft side people might feel fashionable but also incompetent for a while...' 'I'd better do a proper quick GapLeap business case,' he thinks to himself, 'but first...' Al rises to get a glass of water, pausing only to click on an icon to get things started whilst he is away, but instead of opening a light grey dialog box appears. It says:

**This presentation contains content that your browser may not be able to show properly. Please use a more modern browser. Options are 'Download voovle-metallic' or 'Dismiss'**

Al has no idea at all what the message means. Surely a more modern browser would be able to cope with the needs of an older browser? What is it they used to call it? Backward compatibility? Although he doesn't understand the message he understands its implications. He hits the Esc key several times but it's frozen. Somewhere deep inside his chest a scream starts, primeval and throbbing. By the time it reaches his throat it sounds like a bass, grumbling roar, 'Ararrrrghghrgha! Damnit! They've only gone and *improved* it!'

Why oh why oh why don't they find out what *we* do and what improvement looks like to *us* and then innovate to support *us* and help *us* do things which *we* need and want? They push their ideas upon us. Push their ideas of how we should work instead of pulling from us what we want and need. In particular the things which we wish and hope that they would give us but they don't. Instead, when we tell them what we need, which they don't currently give us, they put us into the category of 'obnoxious customers'. As if we're the ones making trouble. They treat us like outliers and ignore our needs. All the effort goes on the less demanding customers, the new ones with no skin in the game, the unsophisticated ones who think they are wonderful and the normal ones who match their focus groups.

That thin smile again. He says to himself, 'I think I'll call John Troy and be generous. I'll not just give him a piece of my mind, I'll give him several large chunks!'

———————————————

*'If you think sunshine brings you happiness,
then you haven't danced in the rain.'*
Anon.

## Chapter 12   The SUSPECT: Me

# Not a Funnel... and Definitely Not a Pipeline...

 My ears are still ringing. John Troy was occupied, busy in a main board meeting so they put the caller through to me as Director of Innovation. I can imagine a customer not wanting new stuff, after all the world is full of Luddites, **but he was complaining about products we were selling to *other* people.** They say the customer is always right but this one I was sure was wrong. And insisting that our innovation should be based on him, his company, his needs, when we have in place an organised pipeline, a very modern divergent/convergent creativity process for creating ideas and a strong stage and gate process to ensure that only the right innovations make it to market. 'Some customers, well some customers,' I think to myself, 'are just a problem.' I shake my head. I can't make any sense of his comments. I wonder what Franck would think.

My thoughts drift. I snuck back into the qubicle and took another look at the notes of our discussion. I then completed Franck's quiz. In ten minutes I am meeting Franck for what he has called a 'drumbeat'. It's a 15-minute update plus Q&A plus action planning session. I've just enough time to get a cup of coffee.

Now I am standing at the whiteboard adding a couple of new 'Hopes' for our next session and waiting for Franck.

'This is impressive – you're right on time.'

'Hi Franck.' I turn my qubot to face his.

'Hello,' he replies, scuttling up to me, past me and up to the whiteboard. 'How are you? Just a couple of new "Hopes"? *"How do I get more, faster out of our innovation pipeline?" "How do I get better ideas from colleagues?"'*

'Fine. Yes,' I reply.

'Let's get on then. Did you manage to complete the quiz I left you last time?'

I point at the completed quiz. A purple laser guides his eyes to the completed quiz.

'Hmmm. Do you know any of the statistics about innovation success?'

I shake my head vigorously, nervous about what is coming next and then remember to speak – 'Errr' – and then shake my qubot's head.

'OK,' he says, combatively, 'to some extent it depends on whose research you believe, but for every product launched guess how many projects were run?'

'About 20,' I guess. 'It's very difficult.'

'Hmmm. OK. Some background. In the 1960s people noticed that in the advertising industry it seemed that the more ideas you had the more likely you were to have a good one. So the simple logic was that the more you put in the more would come out. This led people to invent the innovation-as-a-funnel model. But remember, in delivering to an ad brief the focus was primarily on creativity.'

I'm trying to work out where this is going so I say, 'I don't get your point.'

'You see, the funnel metaphor is fine when you are only looking for occasional innovation as they did in the middle of the last century. I know it's hard to believe but to have a product refresh rate of once every ten years wasn't considered bad at all. The problem starts once you start to use the funnel to manage your 21st-century business in our New World After Midnight.'

He pauses and moves over to my completed quiz, inviting me to join him.

'The first question was "How many ideas do you have which you capture – say by drawing the idea or writing it down?" You said one in ten.'

'Correct.'

'Question 2, "How many of the ideas you capture do you share with a colleague?" You said one in five; for with your boss you said one in three.'

Frank goes through the questions and my answers.

| 1 | How many ideas do you have which you capture – say by drawing the idea or writing it down? | One in 10 |
| 2 | How many of the ideas you capture do you share with a colleague? | One in 5 |
| 3 | How many of the ideas you shared with a colleague do you then share with your boss? | One in 3 |
| 4 | How many of the ideas you have shared get support, resources or funding to take to forward? | One in 8 |
| 5 | How many of the ideas you resource up make it through the organisation's control and management mechanism (funnel pipeline stage-gate)? | One in 20 |
| 6 | How many of those which make it through are successfully launched or rolled out? | One in 3 |
| 7 | How many of the ideas which are launched or rolled out remain in the marketplace or organisation two years later, successfully continuing to provide benefits or profits? | One in 2 |
| Stop at this point and invite your facilitator/tutor to join you | | |
| Answer | Now multiply all the numbers together | |

'Your answer comes out at 1 in 144,000. That's not a pipeline. It's not a normal shaped funnel. It's more like getting a beam of light through a wall!'

I'm stunned. He can't be right. At that rate we'd never generate any innovation in my lifetime. I protest. 'You've got to be wrong – I mean at that pace no one would ever generate any innovation.'

I can feel him smiling as he replies enigmatically, 'And your point is?'

'Well,' I respond prepared to continue my argument, but he cuts across me.

'Just stop and think about what you told me when we first met. *"Everyone seems to want innovation, everyone seems to be supportive of it. They say great things about it but there isn't much of it around."'*

I'm snookered. But I protest, 'One in 144,000?'

'Well if you're really lucky, maybe in *your* organisation there *is* an innovation. Haven't you noticed how all the great songs come from a few writers, how lots of the great inventions come from a few people? I know it's fashionable to believe that the group, through open innovation, can drive innovation but even in an open community there are a couple of nodes who connect and catalyse almost everything that happens.'

'Mark,' I say.

'In that case you'll be fine. But remember, the shelf-life of an innovation in our 21st-century world is often only about two or three years. So you can't survive on ratios of one in a hundred thousand unless your competition is much, much worse than you are. And there is no chance of new entrants to your market. You need to generate a decent **innovation rate**.'

'**Innovation rate**?'

'Yes, the speed with which you replace your revenue from existing offers with new offers. When you work it out as a sum it's the sales revenue (or profits) from innovations developed over the previous three years divided by the total sales (or profits). More than 33% is indefinitely sustainable, more than 15% is probably ok and less than 5% is probably pretty risky.'

I'm trying to make sense of this – 'I wonder what our rate is now,' I mutter under my breath to myself.

'Good question and you've probably realised why I'm not going to address your second hope.'

'About getting colleagues to be more creative?'

'Not until we've understood better how creativity fits in with innovation. And not in the next 20 seconds. And don't worry, we'll soon get round to discussing the HealthCheck as well.'

'Damn!' I say, as I look at my watch. 'Is that the time already? Thanks.'

'But in our New World After Midnight we only travel to be together, for a small set of reasons,' and with that he makes me an offer I can't refuse.

---

*Eagles may soar but turkeys don't get sucked into jet engines.*
*... but they do get caught up in Christmas celebrations every year.*

## Chapter 13   The SUSPECT: The Sales Manager

## Pile 'em High...

 A week to go to the end of the month. A week to go to the end of the quarter. Ten percent to go to hit target. He might not make it and now this. Leonardo Close is fastidiously updating his sales log, tracking through accounts and planning. He's working fast and furiously. He needs to get this done and in his job you know that there are always interruptions. But they aren't interruptions, they are customers. Customers to keep happy with what you've sold them. Customers with service questions which, if you fix them, make you their hero and they'll buy again. Customers who want to buy and need to speak to you so you can remove the last objection. For Leo, a customer is never a problem.

'You've got to make the numbers,' he mumbles to himself. Leo knows that it's not just his livelihood which is at stake. Sure, like most sales people, he recognises that if he doesn't sell he doesn't pay the rent. Simple as that. Sell or starve. Well, not quite starve, but his basic pay is well below his lifestyle. Leo has come to think of himself as a Lion of the Corporate Jungle, wondering when, or if, the next big antelope will cross his path. You never know for sure what you'll make this quarter. Will it be enough to cover your child support? Put good food on your table? Pay unexpected medical bills? Put gas in your new boat? But Leo knows that there is a lot more riding on him selling. He knows that if he doesn't make the numbers the business won't be able to survive.

And now this. His belt vibrates in time to a new message. He scans it. It's a reminder from the Group Sales Director about delivering the targets for the new product and service offers. Leo lets out a loud, slow breath. He's been up since four o'clock that morning and the first thing to dent his motivation has been an internal email.

Non-sales people are always dismissive of sales – they couldn't and wouldn't do it, they couldn't and wouldn't take the rejection, but they act as if it's really easy. It might not be as intricate as engineering, as pressured as IT or as politically challenging as HR, but without sales you won't have a business, not for long. And that is the problem with new fangled innovation offers. He's emailed the team and asked them to give him a brief. Nothing complex: key features and benefits, an exhaustive list of objections and how to overcome them. And he's asked if the marketing support materials and a demonstration are available. They sent him nothing useful so he's met them and that meeting has spooked him. These guys, they are all so positive. They are so excited about their baby that they almost can't believe that a customer will have objections. One of them actually said, 'It's so cool it will practically sell itself'. It's beyond them to recognise that their new offer is not in a vacuum, in isolation, not competing with the other offers which it trumps in features and benefits, but is competing with what the client has and uses now! And that's the toughest sell. He remembers the lesson at sales school where they explained that although 'the grass is always greener...' the human sense of misery at losing what you currently have usually outweighs the potential gain you could get from something new. So even when sticking with the current means that you'll be doomed, human beings cling on to the wreckage of today. When you add to that the risk that something might go wrong with the new offer, and add in the challenge of having to persuade your team, your colleagues or your boss to use it and… He sighs again.

And there is the old adage that it is easiest to sell old stuff to old customers, old stuff to new customers (because you can use testimonials to persuade), new stuff to old customers (because they trust you and will give you the time to explain) and that it is practically impossible to sell new stuff to new clients. This was why all the new, fast-growth businesses hope and pray and rely on peer-to-peer endorsements, word-of-mouth selling through social networks. But no one yet knows the exact formula for getting a social network to do your selling for you. And the challenge is when you sell from one business to another, managers and business people don't often socially network that much. And corporate advantage is still guarded fiercely; so, on finding the coolest piece of software or great equipment supplier, the last thing you are going to do is phone round your competitors to persuade them to use it!

Selling ALCORP's new offer is going to be difficult. The last time there was a major launch he pitched it to some of his best customers. But then the delivery and support schedules slipped and they were late. He'd had to do a lot of tap dancing. He says out loud, 'I need to be certain that it's ready to go before I pitch it'. Leo knows he isn't going to risk selling any of his key customers something he isn't sure of. So that means selling to his less important customers or completely new people where he won't lose so much if it goes wrong. And there isn't enough time to sell to new customers.

The safest thing is to make the numbers and maybe beat them, then we can argue about the mix of products. What he can do in the meantime is to use his old trick. Show the 'shiny new stuff' to a couple of the existing customers, invite the tech support team to help with the tricky questions, demonstrate that you are willing to sell it but close the deal and sell what the customer needs, wants, has bought before and will buy again now. He sighs. Then repeats his mantra to himself, *'The day's not done till the sale is sold. The man's not won till his soul stays bold.'* His back stiffens. He has a plan. And then the phone rings.

———————————————

*Human beings can live without air for a few minutes, without water for a few days, without food for about two months, and without new thoughts for years on end.*

## Chapter 14   The SUSPECT: Me

# Turning (New) Ideas into Money (Society's Benefits)

 ♞. 'Just pull on that chain above your head. Yes, that one. Not too hard, just gently, you don't want to cook the brake pads. Ease off now and then and let them cool. Yes, great. And the most important and stylish thing is to make sure that the rotor comes to rest forward-aft not all skewed and off centre.' ♞. It's not much of a job but I feel the pressure. Franck has just landed and shut down a Robinson helicopter and I now have the responsibility of leaving us looking ship shape. He'd asked me to join him, saying, 'in our World After Midnight the only reason to travel to meet face-to-face was to have a physical experience together like sharing a meal, a drink or a flight, not just to talk. And that's what we'd just done, shared a physical experience.

Brilliant!

Now we are walking back to the hangar. Blue sky with several parallel lines of cloud above us, green everywhere else. The flat field edged with grey shapes of rabbits. A few minutes of paperwork and we're sitting comfortably on the edge of the airfield watching the gliders take off and land in the distance and the rabbits nibble the grass close to our feet.

'Last conversation you were persuading me that innovation was really scarce. I wasn't so sure.'

He laughs. 'Yep, innovation the old-world way is a "mug's game". That's why so many companies are far happier being fast followers than out-and-out innovators. If you can beat the innovator in the marketplace you win. The money without the hassle.'

For me this is sinking in slowly.

'Imagine your organisation has £100,000 to spend on developing and launching innovation ideas. And imagine there was only one idea. Then all that money and your commitment would go into that idea. You would work your way to success or failure, fighting hard at every stage to try to keep it alive and relevant.'

I nod in agreement.

'Now imagine you decide to play the numbers game, asking staff for creative ideas, and so on. You receive 100 ideas, so you only have £1000 to spend on each. There are now far too many to launch properly. Don't you see? The more ideas you generate the more important it is to get the 'right ones' – so the more strict your process and stage-gate has to be to make sure that you don't just waste the money. So you need to cut out the less attractive ideas from the pipeline. But who do you get to sit on the panel to carry out this stringent no-nonsense appraisal? Do you select the executive who is well known for liking wacky, cool, flaky initiatives or the solid, sensible guy, the one who knows the business well?'

I reply confidently, 'The sensible ones of course.'

'So what do you think the sensible, financially astute ones prefer? Ideas they recognise or those they don't?'

I say nothing. My neck feels damp with sweat. I suddenly remember being really pleased when Burt Knox had offered to sit on the Innovation Committee. Now I understand the implications.

Franck hasn't noticed. He continues, 'Is killing off your hard-won ideas,' he pauses briefly, smiling mischievously, 'I mean running your pipeline, free?'

'What do you mean?'

'How much, as a percentage of the cost of the innovation, is running your pipeline for each idea?'

I pause to think. I haven't really considered it. 'I guess there's the admin. The executive time. The database admin. The list goes on...'

'So whichever way you look at it you spend some of your original £100,000 killing off ideas, so chances are you now have less money to spend on the more mediocre ideas which come through. Do you think you have really increased your chances of success over just going with your first idea?'

He has a point.

'So guess what? All that review and stage-gating mean you come to market late with an idea which is similar to what has gone before. In our real world, this new world where change happens faster than we can learn, by the time anything comes out the original situation may have changed beyond recognition.'

I'm stunned again. Again it's just like he's slapped me.

Franck concludes, **'The pipeline/funnel model sends you in the wrong direction. It makes you conclude that the goal is to be creative, but that is not the goal.'**

'But you have to be creative,' I protest. He is attacking my belief system and I react.

'Yes, I agree that you might need to be creative but that's not the goal.' He pauses uncertainly, 'I guess I should check. What do you mean by creativity?'

'Coming up with new ideas,' I say.

'I think of it in a similar way. For me, **creativity is the thinking process that helps us generate ideas and solve "impossible" problems.** Anyway, we're rarely short of ideas. Most people are very creative at the age of eight but learn to hide and suppress their ideas. But in reality there are tons of ideas being generated every second.'

I can sort of see what's coming next.

'From what we've said, do we really need more creativity?'

'But you have to be creative and you have to control the process so it doesn't get out of control,' I say, trying to hold on to my evaporating certainty.

'I've discovered that there is a real confusion between some very different concepts – creativity, invention, design, realisation and innovation. People often use the terms interchangeably.'

'And what's wrong with that?'

'What's wrong is it's impossible to have an executable, aligned strategy for a large number of people if they all interpret what they are trying to deliver in several different ways.'

'It's just semantics.'

Franck cuts across me saying, 'I thought you told me your organisation needed to evolve to deliver sustainable innovation.'

I nod.

'Why does your organisation need to evolve to deliver sustainable innovation?'

'To survive in that New World After Midnight we discussed?'

'And what is the key arbiter of life or death in a business organisation?'

I barely miss a beat. 'Making money,' I reply quickly.

'So is there any point in being creative, designing, realising a project, or invention in your situation if it doesn't make money?'

'Err. No,' I reply, 'I guess not,' wondering why he left the word innovation out of his previous list.

'Have you found it really easy to sell new innovations?

'No, it's been quite difficult.'

'Why is that?'

'Well, the existing customers don't really want something new to replace what they have.'

Franck nods. 'I see, but why don't you sell to new customers?'

'Well, sales usually start off the rounds with their key accounts.'

'And sales really know the needs of these key accounts so I don't understand why they don't point you to customers who really want your innovation.'

I pause, thinking. And it slips out silently, 'I guess because they don't really want to.' And then it dawns on me, 'selling the innovation disrupts their targets and also introduces something new and uncertain into their key relationships. Sales haven't bought in. And if they don't, we can't turn the idea into money.' I'm lost in a stream of unpleasant thoughts.

Franck interrupts them, 'What's the word for the process of turning (new) ideas into money (society's benefits)?'

I shrug.

He smiles and says, 'I'll give you a clue it starts with an "I".'

I respond flatly, 'Are you trying to get me to say innovation?'

I can feel the warmness of his smile.

I decide to get my own back. 'Yes, innovation does start with an "I"… an Idea!' We both laugh.

He then adds darkly, '…and ends in Ignominy. Thing is, people don't value ideas enough. If the ideas were more tangible, frail looking and cuddly,' he pauses for a second, points and says, 'like one of those rabbits. Yes, if each of your ideas was like one of those cuddly-wuddly-bubbly rabbits you wouldn't want any harm to come to them would you?'

'No,' I say, looking at the grey mounds of fur nearby.

'But this is what you do. You plan to send the rabbits on a journey – just like with innovation – the idea travels all the way to money. Your rabbits have to make it from this field all the way to the centre of town.' He pauses, appearing to think, '…where there's a "Rabbit of the Year Show" with prizes and lettuce leaves.'

I nod, to show I'm following him but I'm actually wondering where he is going with this.

'What you guys do is you assemble 144,000 rabbits and shoo them off. Whoa! Go! Go! Go! And they start to hop, hop off towards town. They reach the runway and splat! Some of them get squished by the landing gliders, some make it to the woods beyond and the foxes catch some of them and rip out their throats, blood everywhere.' He is delivering this fast-paced, barely pausing to breathe, waving his arms wildly to indicate the blood splattering all around and is clearly enjoying the fantasy he is creating. 'Past the farmhouse. Bang! Bang! The farmer, like your stage-gate committee, kills dozens for the pot. Across the motorway. Thud! Thud! Thud! Then into the town where the animal control operative gasses and poisons them… Finally one, one out of 144,000 rabbits arrives at the "Rabbit of the Year Show," fur covered in blood and full of holes,' he pauses and then adds as a punctuation, 'limping!' That, my friend, is what your innovation process looks like.'

He sits back triumphantly.

I sit back stunned.

A moment passes in silence.

'How else could you do it?' he challenges. 'How could you make sure more rabbits arrived safely?'

'Start with even more of them?' I offer.

'Oh dear,' he says, 'we're back to the 'more creativity is the solution' mindset. Even more cruelty to even more rabbits.'

It smarts. I'm hurt by his comment. I stall.

'Come on,' he urges.

'We could stop the gliders landing,' I offer tentatively.

'Not so easy with gliders,' he says smiling, 'but you could patrol the runway only letting the rabbits across when it was safe. What else?'

'We could shoo away the foxes and stop the farmer shooting them!' Now I'm on a roll.

'Fantastic thought. You could stop shooting your own ideas, get rid of the innovation stage-gate approvals committee.'

I wince.

'Yes,' he says, 'with this type of World After Midnight thinking, you will need far fewer rabbits and it makes sense to use the time and energy freed up to breed tough, fast rabbits that can make the journey and win the prizes at the show.'

'Tough, fast rabbits?' I repeat, trying to work out if he's teasing me.

'Tough as in resilient enough to get through the corporate politics, fast as in not getting stuck in the treacle of change and being rapidly accepted by the end users.' He pauses and then adds, '...with sharp teeth.' He throws back his head and laughs raucously.

'Shh,' I say, ' you're frightening the **rabbits**,' as I notice them bolting down their holes.

'Sorry.'

We rise and walk to the car park to drive back to work and normal life. As we walk, Franck reaches into his coat pocket and fishes out a deck of cards in a transparent plastic box which he hands to me. The top card of the deck has a drawing of a magician standing in a giant hat and has the word 'Innovation' and Franck's signature.

'Wait a second and open it when I'm gone.' He shakes my hand and jumps into a dark green car and leaves.

I open the plastic box take the deck out. At the bottom of the box there is a shiny silver ring to thread through the holes punched neatly in the top left hand corner of each card. I push the ring through the holes and clip it shut and begin to turn the cards over. The second card says '*R.A.B.B.I.T. The Journey to Innovation.*'

I grin. I thought he'd made up the **rabbit** story just for me but he's told it before – often enough to have created a set of cards about it. And then I realise why he'd invited me to go flying. I realise why he'd wanted us to meet at the airfield where hundreds of **rabbits** live. He wanted the story to feel true, to resonate and stick with me, stick firmly in my mind. I stand in the middle of the car park turning over card after card. Here was the 'Hopes&Fears' tool he'd used on QUBE. This one said 'Evolve, Dominate or Die'. This was the weblink ❀ to the HealthCheck I'd filled in but we'd not discussed…

———————————————

*'Everyone thinks that people who do unsafe, dangerous things are dare-devils, risk takers but they are wrong, people who do unsafe things have to be very safe indeed if they are to survive!'*
Quentin Smith[7]

## Chapter 15   The SUSPECT: The Team Member

# Who Do You Dance with when the Party Is Over?

 'It's all very well for Mark, but how about the rest of us?' Ted Edison thinks moodily to himself hunched over a desk on the third floor. Project Integration Team is embossed on the pad of paper which sits ignored in the middle of his desk. 'I gave up a secure position in the organisation to participate in this project. It was supposed to be the future of the organisation and now...' His thoughts trail off into nothingness. The problem was the culture of the organisation. Always someone had to be to blame and people seemed so in love with and passionate about the triumphs of the past you almost seemed to insult them if you suggested that there might be a better or more modern way. Would the team be disbanded? Would he be able to find another role in the organisation with the new headcount freeze on? Would another project come along quickly enough?

It hasn't been easy, being a full time member of the team. Everyone else in the organisation has viewed us with suspicion

---

7    Quentin Smith – Round the world helicopter pilot and the first person to fly a piston engined machine to the South Pole. 🎥 You may have seen him land a helicopter on a moving car on Top Gear. Start video at 5 minutes. 🎥

for the past three months. Acted as if we have set ourselves up as some sort of elite club. He protests audibly, 'We haven't! It's just that we were a bit closer to what was going on.' The resentment was completely unjustified and now it will probably be followed by gloating. How stupid. The project was supposed to be the future of the business – not just their future, everybody's future. Mark had said that over and over again. They were ahead of the competition for once. So of course there wasn't any focus group or market data to support the investment. The market didn't have a clue what was coming next. They had only stumbled upon the opportunity because they had taken the time, patience and humility to listen to the very, very small band of opinionated but disgruntled customers who couldn't understand why in this day and age they couldn't get the services they really needed. Most of the organisation simply labelled such customers as troublemakers and obnoxious, and were happy and keen to see the back of them. The team had realised that this small band of people were in fact explaining precisely what the future would look like and that was the source of the insight. The source of the breakthrough innovation... and now...

---

*Three guys, stranded on a desert island, find a magic lantern containing a genie, who grants each of them one wish. The first guy wishes he was off the island and back home. The second guy wishes the same. The third guy says, 'I'm lonely. I wish my friends were back here'.*

## Chapter 16   The SUSPECT: Me

## Why Doesn't It Just Happen?

'The other strange thing is that innovation seems to generate some sort of amnesia in people who have been innovative. It's almost as if, having visited the Gods once, the door closes behind you. It leads to the one-hit-wonder situation where for example in music many artists create real breakthroughs, make a lot of money and then after that all their music is simply derivative. Corporations do this too. They have one successful breakthrough product and they spend all their efforts creating variants of the original successful formula. It's almost the opposite of your funnel process where the funnel is upside down and from one idea many similar variants are sent along the red-carpeted stage-gate process!'[8]

I'm listening to Franck from home this time. I've become used to seeing his boxy avatar scuttling around the qubicle. I'd snuck in to look around the qubicle we had been meeting in but he had seen me go on QUBE from his notifier and had joined me. Now he's just put on the screen a slide which shows a set of pictures of many variants of the SONY Walkman above a set of pictures showing a range of variants of ipods. I search for ALCORP's

8    With Thanks to Sandy McDowell, Amadeus.

offer brochure pdf, open it and share my screen with him. 'If you can produce enough variants you create a corporate division where more-of-the-same, or actually more-of-almost-the-same-with-minute-variations, rules. The Model T Ford but in several shades of black! There is product and offer proliferation but no breakthrough innovation.

'I guess it's the same where you are,' he remarks flatly.

'Yes, but why does this happen?'

He chuckles. 'It's all to do with Sparqs.'

'Quarks? What do subatomic particles have to do with our product portfolio?'

'No, I said Sparqs.' He pauses. 'There are several ways – no, sources, or to put it better, sparks – by which the gem of the idea comes about. Look,' he says, sounding frustrated at how difficult he is finding it to explain his thoughts simply. He drags an image of the sort of sign you get outside a restaurant offering the 'dish of the day'. 'You see, people have to eat every day. It gets a bit boring and repetitive so some ideas arise from creating a (new) way to satisfy a (potential) human need. Now there's a picture of a pot of modelling clay. You have or have developed a resource of technology. What can you turn it into which will be useful? In other words, you have to find a use for a technology/capability you have (developed). These types of Sparqs of ideas come from you, out of your organisation, out of your mind, and you push them out into the world hoping they'll fit. What,' he asks, 'is the danger with these **push Sparqs**? Where does it go wrong for them?'

I think for a second and then it's obvious. 'You discover no-one wants what you're offering. I guess you have to push really hard if people don't want your idea.'

His qubot nods and another picture appears, this time of an old-style penny farthing next to a modern drop-handle track bike. 'Riding a penny farthing was exhilarating right up to the point you fell off and died,' he says, 'then someone looked at the existing technology and found a way to make it "better" and safer using gears.' Then he puts up a picture of a puzzled-looking Santa Claus. 'Ever wondered what to buy for someone which they actually want or need? Sometimes you have to get a bit sneaky observing human behaviour to find a real human need and finding a way to satisfy it. These two seem to come from the opposite direction. More of a pull. So where is the danger for these types of Sparqs?'

This is trickier and then I get it. 'Not invented here. There is no department responsible for taking on board customer quirks...'

'**Push Sparqs generally get the thumbs down from outside the organisation. Pull Sparqs get rejected by the organisation because they don't fit the current structure and KPIs**, which if you think about it you'll realise were both designed for yesterday. You can always tell the innovative health of an enterprise by creating a Sparq map of the four types,' he says dragging up a slide with four quadrants.

'We'd definitely be unbalanced. Almost every innovation project we've done has been based on our views of how to improve the current offer. Techno-Push I think you called it? I guess that's why we have so much trouble getting the customers to take up our innovations...' I stop mid-sentence as the shock of realisation hits me. The words 'on board' leave my mouth but my mind is filled with my recollection of the phone call from Al King the irate customer who 'wanted us to develop our innovations around his needs.'

'What?' asks Franck, noticing me stumble over my words.

'Oh, nothing,' I reply. And trying to deflect his inquiry I say, 'I've still not worked out what to do about your rabbits.'

'Not much you can do,' he replies. 'Once you've understood the model it's all pretty obvious.'

'Yes,' I reply, then pause. 'What's obvious?'

'The fact that in innovation the only way to succeed is to identify the places where the rabbits are most vulnerable – this will be a sort of bottleneck – and then to put all your effort into saving the rabbits at that stage. For every rabbit you save one more will make it to the Event.'

'Yeah,' I say, trying to sound cool. 'And where are these places?'

🎥 'Hang on,' he says and then he drags a document off the shelf onto the big virtual screen. 🎥 It's a terrifying image. A

tangled mess of arrows, lines and oval bubbles. 'This is the
BubbleDiagram™ I developed when I worked out where the
Sparqs get killed.'

'Bubble diagram? It looks more like a Bolognaise Diagram
covered in spaghetti,' I remark looking at the mess.

He laughs loudly. 'Not only are there no straight lines in
nature, all the world's simple linear problems were solved years
ago. All the problems that remain today are multi-causality,
interdependent, self-reinforcing nightmares. For every complex
problem there is a simple representation... and it's wrong!' 📷

'Err.'

But he doesn't wait for me to gather my thoughts. 'Let me zoom
in for you... here.' He zooms round the diagram reading it as
he goes. '"*Our key innovation champions leave*" so "*there is
a loss of momentum*" and this "*convinces the sceptics that
innovation was a bad idea in the first place*"... "*The financial
controllers are worried about the returns on what looks like*

*risky speculation"* so *"they make sure that they are involved in the process."* *"We haven't understood the customers' real needs"* and *"we have no real insights to customer behaviour"* so *"we develop an offer which doesn't quite fit"* so *"we have to promote or discount our offer heavily to get it sold."* Because *"the product doesn't resonate with the customers"* *"our sales team are reluctant to put the new innovation in front of their most important customers"...'*

I get it. It's some sort of messy cause–effect diagram.

'And that's how we know that there are five common anchors,' he concludes. He swooshes another diagram onto the screen. This one is legible. 'What you need to find out is where the rabbits,' then he corrects himself, 'or Sparqs get killed in your organisation and who is killing them. Once you know that we can focus. We can involve all the stakeholders, teach them new skills and ways of working, get them to collaborate and deliver not just an innovation culture but real tangible results in no time. And for a start we can use the results of the HealthCheck you completed. It will tell you, from your point of view, where to focus our efforts. Once we have improved the bottleneck and started to get innovation flowing we will set up an innovation "farm" for breeding our tough, fast rabbits.

'And remember, in our world after midnight we understand that you get the best, not through instruction or checking, but by empowering people and giving them the means and tools to see for themselves how cool what they are working on is. Look at the *Achieving Focus* set in your card deck for clues,' he says.

Now it's my turn to sit back in my chair and smile and smile and smile.

---

*'We can easily forgive a child who is afraid of the dark; the real tragedy of life is when men are afraid of the light.'*
Plato

## Chapter 17   The SUSPECT: The Supplier

## Zero Sum Game

'More paperwork.' Jose Molina is sitting at a cluttered desk opposite an intern. He reads the letter. 'We are updating our supplier database to include all our preferred and key suppliers. In order for you to be considered to be included in this list you will need to complete the attached forms...' He leafs through the pages, tutting as he turns each one over. He turns to the intern to deliver a lecture. 'Sales. Sales used to be the big thing and then a while ago someone noticed that ninety percent of what came in went out again, so they decided that they should focus on what their organisations bought. And with that came "professionalised" purchasing and enterprise logistics and supply chain systems and the rest of the story, where the organisations cement themselves into complex, unyielding processes and systems, is history.' But now the story he is telling is his present. Jose is bemused. For a start, the professionalised purchasers keep treating him in the same way as they treat all the other suppliers. True, some suppliers only provide the same commodities that others produce but in his case it's different. Sure he should be on the key suppliers list but, if that's so, why do the customers insist on writing the requests for proposals and project briefs themselves? Most of the time what they are asking for is unintelligible or wrong. He has to do a delicate dance to get them on the right track. It's delicate because they insist on fixed deadlines, refuse to respond to additional questions and insist on all sorts of pointless activities which make it impossible to **learn what they need** rather than go along with **what they think they want**. 'You know,' he says, 'six months ago ALCORP decided to put the services we provide to them out to reverse auction, e-auction. We decided not to take part. Guess how many suppliers made proposals that would work as a replacement to us?'

The intern stares and guesses, 'Five?'

Jose puts his index finger to his thumb forming a circle. 'Zero. It was brilliant for us. The next quarter we raised our prices by 10%. Shame for them. They set off to reduce their costs but because they "know the cost of everything and the value of nothing" they couldn't see the difference between strategic or innovative suppliers and everyone else, and since they only have a single process for buying everything…' His voice grows louder and higher as he speaks.

'But they've not learned anything from that experience. All this form-filling costs. I hope they've done a business case on it. It costs them to produce it and send it out. And if I have to fill all this in…' he pauses to leaf through the stapled pile of paper again, 'the costs will simply end up on my bill to them. And I suspect it's the same for all the other quality suppliers. And that's where you come in,' he says turning to the intern. 'To keep the costs to the client down you are going to complete these accurately. Without me needing to check them. So in a way you're not working for me, you're working for ALCORP.'

The intern smiles nervously, not sure what to make of the challenge.

But Jose is now on a roll. 'And what's even worse is that I know that if ALCORP was a bit more trusting, modern and

collaborative in working with suppliers they would discover
easy ways to save themselves much more time and cost. At the
moment our credit checker tells me that they are strapped for
cash. Now here's a story. My brother who runs a paint business
used to sell paint to the facilities managers of tower blocks. In
tough times it became harder and harder to sell paint. With cash
flow tight the landlords couldn't afford such big capital outlays
but were liable for the external appearance of the buildings.
And the tenants complain bitterly if the landlord doesn't
maintain the appearance. So now he guarantees the look of the
tower blocks on a service level agreement for a fixed monthly
amount. He's happy since he can forward plan and the landlords
are happy because they don't have to find big lumps of cash.
It's transformed his business model and theirs to everyone's
advantage.'

The intern nods but asks, 'What's a **business model**?'

'It's the second of five questions you ask about an enterprise. It's
"How do we intend to make money?" If you want to transform
the enterprise you look for ideas, new ideas which you can use
to change how you make money. My brother has moved from
having customers give him money for tangible goods to being
given money for risk removal, a sort of, call it an insurance
policy.'

'Oh, I see,' says the intern thoughtfully.

'I know I could do the same for ALCORP in many different
ways. Even in packaging I know how they store and use our
materials – we could easily change how we package, that is the
number of units, and make things much easier at their end. In
fact we could provide the initial services in that area far more
effectively than they can. But all they focus on is trying to get
the cost down.' He stares at the intern for a second. 'My business

school Prof., Franck, always used to say, "Never forget Jose, VeeBeeCee!"'

The intern stares back uncertainly, saying nothing.

'Go on, ask me.'

'What is V, B, C?' he asks meekly.

'That's better. In business never be afraid to ask. Hiding your ignorance is a game for civil servants and functionaries to play. For a real business person or entrepreneur questions are gold. **Value** is equal to **Benefits** minus the **Costs. Value is the goal, not cost reduction,** and **you can squeeze out more value by adding benefits as well as by reducing costs.**'

'I don't understand,' says the intern in a more confident voice.

'Imagine ALCORP allowed me to find the value in the interstices between our businesses by making their process five percent more effective. They'd be ahead of the game even if I raised our prices by two percent. And we'd both be happy and that,' he pauses for effect, 'means **getting innovation from your key suppliers is not a** zero sum game.'

The intern's face lights up as the understanding dawns.

'The problem is that everyone reads the same books and literature and most of the modern literature is derivative, that is, one author simply copying and regurgitating what another author has written, so it fools us into thinking that because we've heard the same idea from several sources it must be correct and verified and proven. And one thing you hear over and over again is that customers and clients are *the* source of innovation so many organisations and businesses make the same mistake.'

'What mistake is that?'

'You must never allow arguments you read in books to replace your own thinking!'

The intern giggles.

'When they are looking for innovation they all look for insights to their customers or clients – it's like a row of people with their heads all turned to the left trying to help the person on their left who ignores them, completely preoccupied by looking to their left! The mistake they make is not to look to their suppliers as a free and incredibly effective source of innovation.'

'I see what you mean.'

'I guess what ALCORP don't realise is that these days the customer is no longer king. The right customer is king and by trying to get us to commoditise what we do for them instead of demanding the most innovative and money-making solution for both of us, they stop being a priority customer. The priority customer I'm looking for is a **demanding customer who will keep us innovating**, understand that the **process is a partnership** between us and them, and help to de-risk it and have **great brand name** so I can use them for testimonials.' He smiles, sits forward and hands the huge sheaf of paper to the intern.

*My boss says that in these challenging times we're going to have to do the work of three. We're going to have to be focused, work smarter, be inventive and creative. Thank goodness there are five of us in the team.*

## Chapter 18   The SUSPECT: Me

# Who Dunnit?

That was an hour and a half I'll never forget. My 'full presentation' of an hour and a half to explain what had happened to our best chance innovation felt and ran just like the final scene from a Hercule Poirot movie.

I'd invited extra guests to the presentation – one of the team members of the star innovation project, Leonardo Close from Sales, Al King, one of our key customers and Jose Molina, our key and most creative supplier.

First I'd explained about innovation in the World After Midnight. This was the preamble letting them know why killing the Sparq was such a heinous crime. Then, as I metaphorically twiddled my moustache, I'd explained how each and every one of us had a vested interest in killing off innovation. This was a tricky part – I could see the executives shifting uncomfortably in their seats as I described how everyone wanted innovation until it came to contributing or, more importantly, changing their behaviour or their staff's KPIs. At one point I thought John was going to fire me on the spot. That was the point at which I invited Al King to speak. It broke the tension hearing from one of our longest-standing and most valuable customers. And then when Jose Molina told the execs just how much money he could save us whilst saving himself the same amount the mood changed completely. With the audience on my side I could now explain how, by thinking and acting in line with the real world, the World After Midnight and not the traditional business environment we'd all grown up in, we wouldn't have any reasons to try to kill the Sparq.

Now the ExCo were happy to speak and openly share their concerns and questions on how we could become more aligned to the World After Midnight. I let this discussion run for ten minutes and then I put up a slide of the five key places where Sparqs of ideas got killed. It was just a large picture of one of Franck's deck of cards.

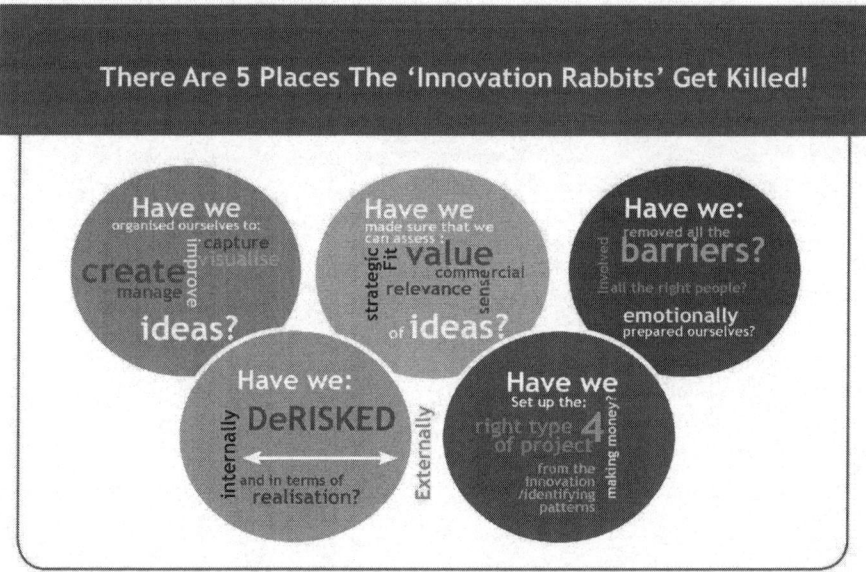

We discussed our views on the most dangerous one of the five places for our Sparqs and discovered our bottleneck. Once we had agreed on the area to focus on, or in my role as Poirot what I now thought of and described as 'The Culprit', I took the deck of cards out of my jacket pocket, placed them on the table and selected the set of relevant cards. I handed them round so everyone could see, in a concrete way, precisely what we needed to do differently to succeed with future innovation. Then I took a deep breath and revealed the final part of my plan. I had persuaded Franck to allow us to use QUBE for learning a new way of working and for connecting all the key people from around the world.

🎥 I showed them round the qubicle Franck had coached me in, sharing the videos and explaining all the performance enhancement tools he had introduced me to. 🎥

And now it was over.

---

*'Sparqs which catch alight illuminate the world.'*
Eddie Obeng

## Chapter 19   The SUSPECT: Everyone

# The Other End

'So alive.' His qubot head nods up and down as he moves his mouse forwards and backwards to signal to all the other people present that he is delighted with progress. 'Energised. Somehow...' his voice trails off. In the qubicle it is still daytime through the windows even though for him the winter afternoon has now turned to dark night in the window behind him. The large oak table at which he sits faces into the room and above the head of his orange qubot is his name plaque which proclaims in white on orange that this is John Troy CEO.

On the slate in front of John is a report. A report from me. A report on our current innovation rate, how we have used a mixed strategy of 'big I' strategic innovation and all inclusive (staff customers, suppliers and many more), campaign-driven 'little i' innovation to improve the bottom line and the top line in just four months. To make the 'little i' innovation take off I've disbanded the stage-gate committee and empowered the people who come up with ideas to share them, improve them and get them over Franck's 5 Bunny Hops. This means that, although we get fewer ideas coming through, the ones we do have good business cases and have engagement from the potential end users. So we feel confident to spend resources on making them happen. At over five hundred thousand bucks of profit per page John should be riveted, caught up in the detail and arguments. Instead, he whispers to himself softly, 'I'm sure we've set out on a journey which means more than just the numbers.' And then unexpectedly he says out loud excitedly, 'Definitely so alive. I am so happy that we had the courage to go for real business transformation instead of just saying the words and killing the Sparq. I am so happy that we understood the concept of Learn+Do Ware – I mean this QUBE,' he pauses, distracted, 'and I love the yellow in this qubicle. This initiative of getting all our key people to participate or be mentors in Franck's innovation community on QUBE, hub-Q has really changed our culture and the ways we do things day to day. I…' his voice trails off. Now he's lost in happy thoughts.

Across the qubicle there are about fifty other people represented by qubots in a rainbow of colours. A group of ALCORP executives are sitting on beanbags in the corner of the room lost in a deep discussion. For three of them from Asia it's bedtime whilst for the Brazilian and Canadian it's almost breakfast.

At a huge whiteboard to the right of the window there is a group of managers, ALCORP customers and a supplier working together. Half of them are using one of Franck's tools, a Pentacle performance enhancement tool as he likes to call them or PET for short. This PET called GapLeap™ is to help them create a complete business case in 15 minutes for a completely new innovation with no track record. From a distance they seem to be about five minutes in. The other half are also working on a PET called SlizedBred™. Their job is to make sure that they have taken onboard all the objections that any future customer will have, as early as possible into development. Three US-based clients will be along in a couple of hours, once everyone has left, to look at what is being proposed and leave their comments.

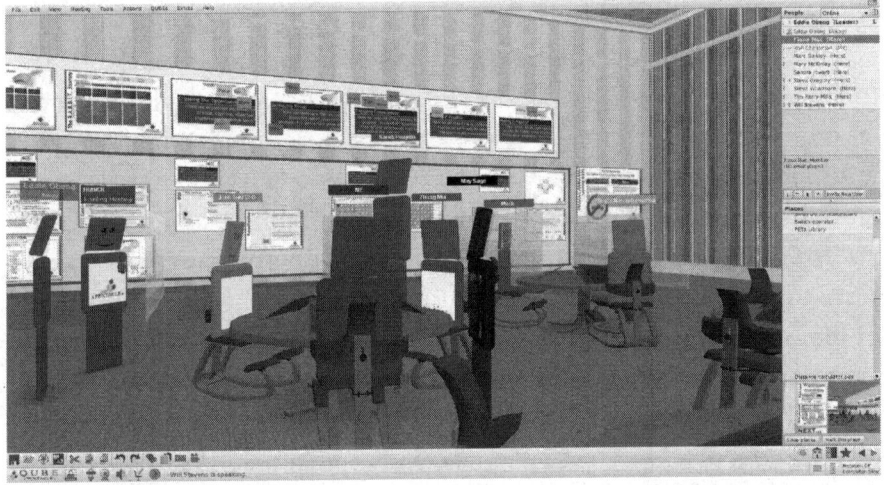

In the main area of the qubicle half a dozen people are looking at a huge projector screen. The presenter, whose qubot is just below the screen, is talking through the feedback from some early prototypes. Their discussion is being facilitated by Gupta of McKlaskeys. Franck has made sure that there is expert facilitation and has trained up five people from McKlaskeys and ten from ALCORP to be able to facilitate virtual events. Funnily enough, one of the disciplines which we routinely use on QUBE, SpinCasting™ (a process for involving everyone in a conversation by rotating who speaks), we now find ourselves using even when we're not working virtually.

I walk up to John, seated at the oak table. He looks up at me and turns on his webcam. Instantly the qubot's head switches from showing a still smiley to showing a live stream of John's head and shoulders in his office.

His real head is also smiling. 'How's Mark getting on?'

I reply positively, 'Looks like the Sparqs are all safe.'

He nods for real and as a qubot. 'But I'm in big trouble. I promised **Them** that there would be a result, a big result, a result to show that we could take on the global challenge of low-price labour and win. But now they want to know how we're doing it and it's almost impossible to explain. You try talking about "rabbits" at a main board meeting and see what happens to your credibility. And when I try to **explain** QUBE **and how we have transformed our business to be completely without boundaries of ideas, time zones, departments, new learning and application, they just don't get it**. But the worst is when they ask what QUBE is or what a senior guy like me is doing "playing at being an avatar," it's too hard to explain so I just point at the balance sheet and the double-digit growth. Anyway, what are you doing this weekend?'

'I think my other half has me down to help with the gardening,' I reply brightly. 'How about you?'

'Well, I've started my Master Yachtsman course. It's to qualify me to sail boats of up to 100 feet.'

---

*PART TWO:*

*THE CULPRIT*

I've attached the deck of cards Franck gave me. They are good triggers and aides-memoires and if you want to know more you can click on them…

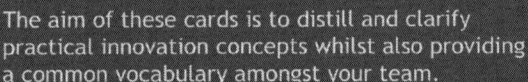

INNOVATION

The aim of these cards is to distill and clarify
practical innovation concepts whilst also providing
a common vocabulary amongst your team.

Just rifle through the cards or use the
categories provided to help you structure them.

Pin

File

Categorise

# R.A.B.B.I.T*

## The Journey To InnoVatiOn

*By Eddie Obeng with Christophe Gillet, Andy Burnett, Colin Burns, David Lomas,

## R.A.B.B.I.T™

### Why R.A.B.B.I.Ts?

I like to imagine new ideas - the sparks of innovation as rabbits... soft, fluffy, delicate rabbits. Easily killed by treacherous roads and foxes. The task is to get your rabbits from A to B - from idea to money.

In the Old World - we believed that if we bred loads of rabbits, then it didn't matter whether some got squashed or eaten or shot (possibly even by you!) - one rabbit would get to its destination eventually, and that is all we needed!

In the New World - we prefer to breed the very best rabbits. Look out for the strongest, fastest, happiest rabbits, nurture them, feed them well, and go along the journey with them - looking out for danger and keeping them on course. Rabbits are happy and enriched along the way and the result is far better, far quicker and far more profitable. At the end, we have far more rabbits who have survived the journey. **Make sure you protect your rabbits from the biggest dangers.**

You can find more on this subject at:
PentaclePets.com/RABBIT.htm

**2**

## Evolve, Dominate or Die

### In the New World - there are only 3 choices:

**EVOLVE?**

Constantly changing, growing and dreaming, inventing… **INNOVATING**

**DOMINATE?**

Stay ahead of the game, do what it takes to stay on top, fight for, drive and maintain your top spot

**DIE?**

Do nothing, go nowhere, sit and take it, fold under the pressure to survive or sell-up and live on your huge yacht

innovative - being or producing something like nothing done or experienced or created before; "stylistically innovative works"; "innovative members of the artistic community"; "a mind so innovational, so original"

innovation:
a new method, idea, product…
Generation of new or improved products and services
Characterized by the creation of new ideas or things; Forward looking; ahead of current thinking
The act of innovating; the introduction of something new, in customs, rites, etc; A change effected by innovating; a change in customs; something new, and contrary to established customs, manners, or rites; A newly formed shoot, or the annually produced addition to the stems of many mosses

The act of innovating; it means of economic growth; increasing value; something new; change; thinking; radical, and creative…

The innovation is a measure of something. It means…
In signal processing, the innovation is the difference between the observed value of a variable at time t and the optimal forecast of that value based on information available prior to time t. …

# I<sub></sub>N**O**VA**T**I**O**N?

# =

## The process of turning (NEW) ideas into money or benefits*

**\* The Rabbit's Journey**

## Eddie's Favourite Statistics

**75%**
**78,450**
**23%**
1,760,000
<1/100,000

* **Fraction of perfect projects**
* Number of Google hits for: innovation + change + consultant
* **Strategic acquisitions which don't meet their targets**
* **Books in Amazon on 'Creativity' and 'Innovation'**
* Rabbits which make it!

## Old World Model        New World Reality

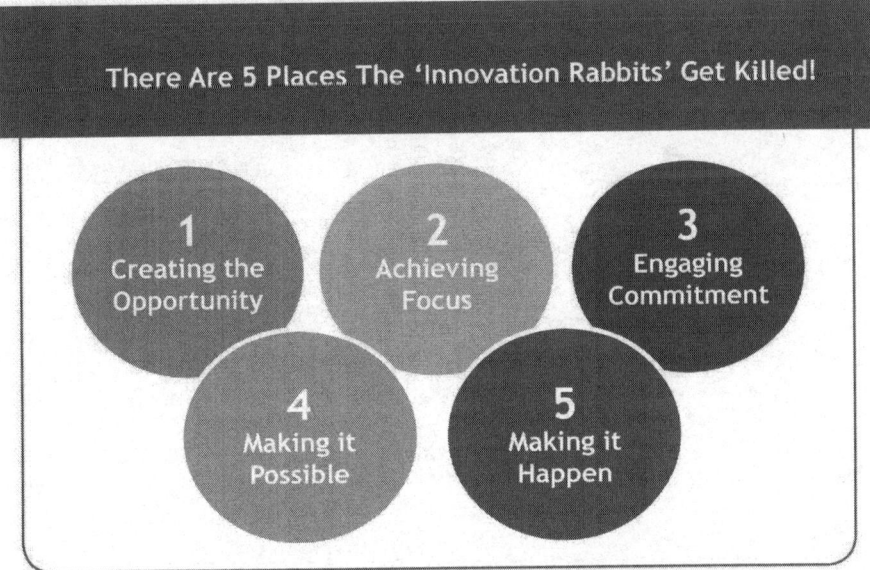

There Are 5 Places The 'Innovation Rabbits' Get Killed!

1 Creating the Opportunity

2 Achieving Focus

3 Engaging Commitment

4 Making it Possible

5 Making it Happen

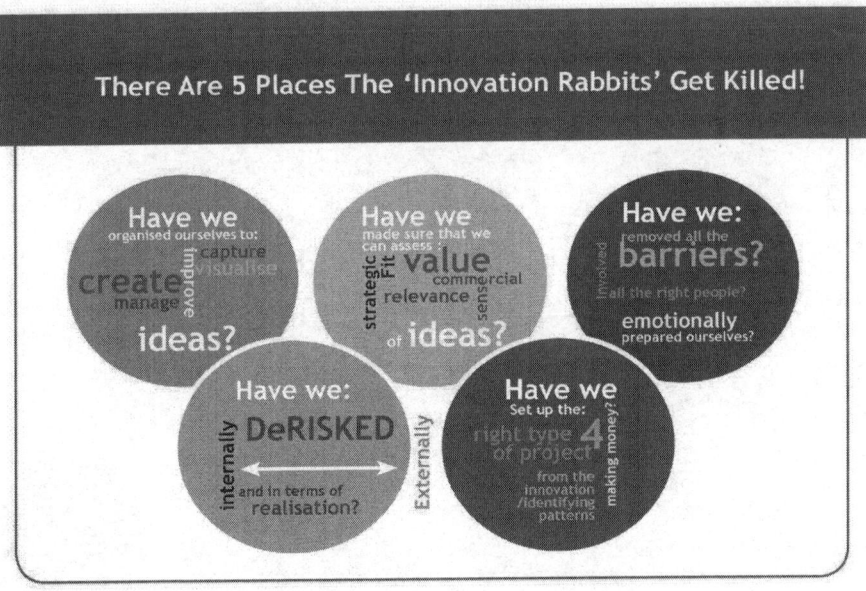

There Are 5 Places The 'Innovation Rabbits' Get Killed!

Have we: organised ourselves to: improve capture visualise create manage ideas?

Have we: made sure that we can assess strategic Fit value commercial relevance sense of ideas?

Have we: removed all the barriers? involved all the right people? emotionally prepared ourselves?

Have we: internally DeRISKED Externally and in terms of realisation?

Have we Set up the: right type of project from the innovation /identifying patterns making money?

## Where Do Your Rabbits Get Killed?

# Take our free quiz

PentacleTheVBS.com/Innovation_Healthcheck.htm

And write your scores on the back of the card...

## Write Your Scores Here

Score

_____

Score

_____

Score

_____

Score

_____

Score

_____

9

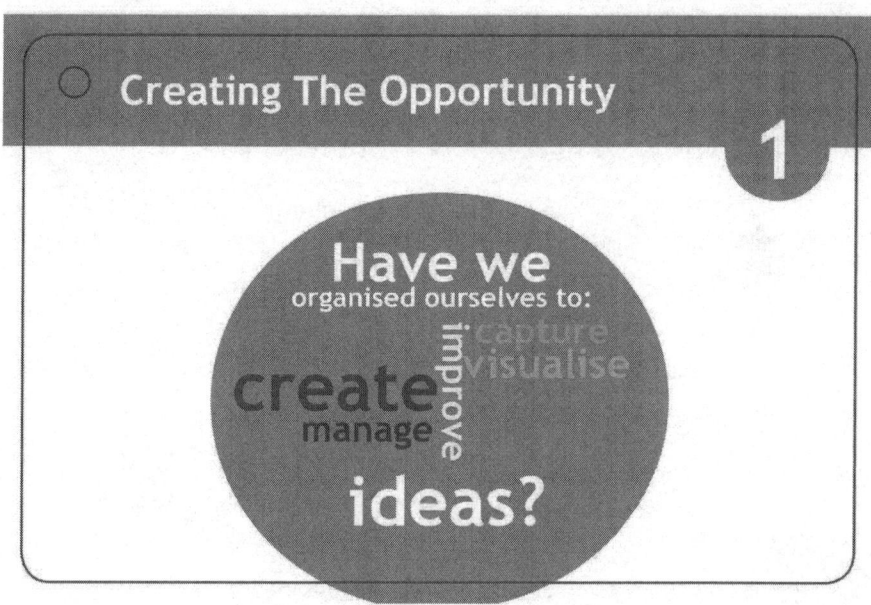

Creating The Opportunity

1

Have we organised ourselves to: improve capture visualise create manage ideas?

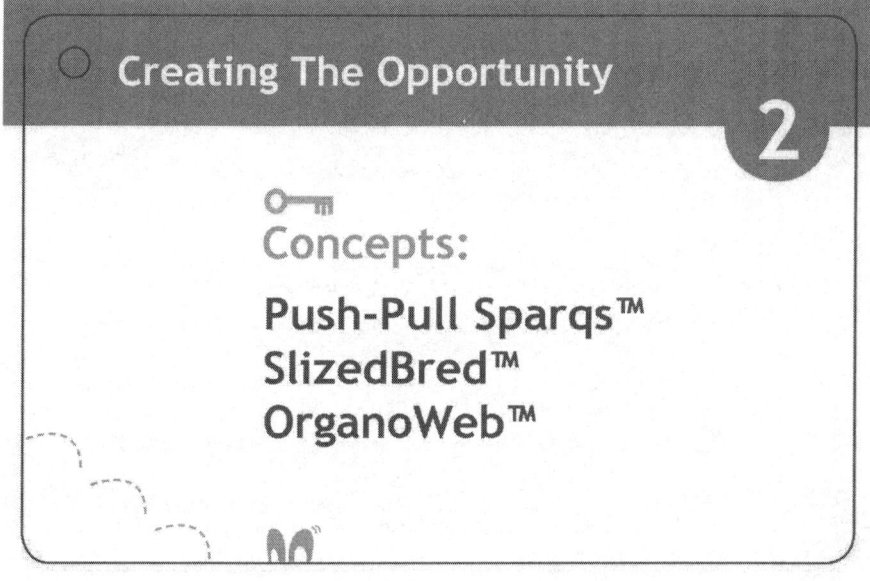

Creating The Opportunity

2

Concepts:

**Push-Pull Sparqs™**
**SlizedBred™**
**OrganoWeb™**

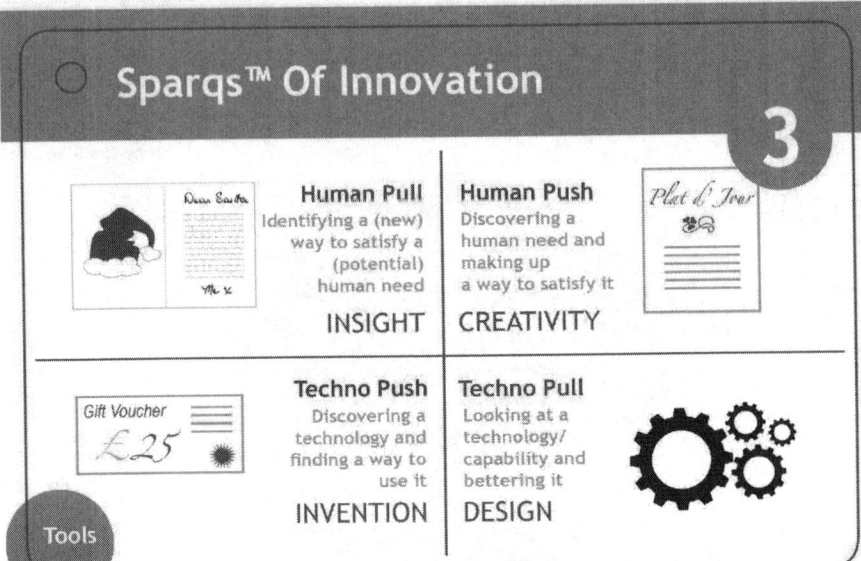

## Sparqs™ Of Innovation

**3**

| | | |
|---|---|---|
| **Human Pull**<br>Identifying a (new) way to satisfy a (potential) human need<br><br>**INSIGHT** | **Human Push**<br>Discovering a human need and making up a way to satisfy it<br><br>**CREATIVITY** | |
| **Techno Push**<br>Discovering a technology and finding a way to use it<br><br>**INVENTION** | **Techno Pull**<br>Looking at a technology/ capability and bettering it<br><br>**DESIGN** | |

Tools

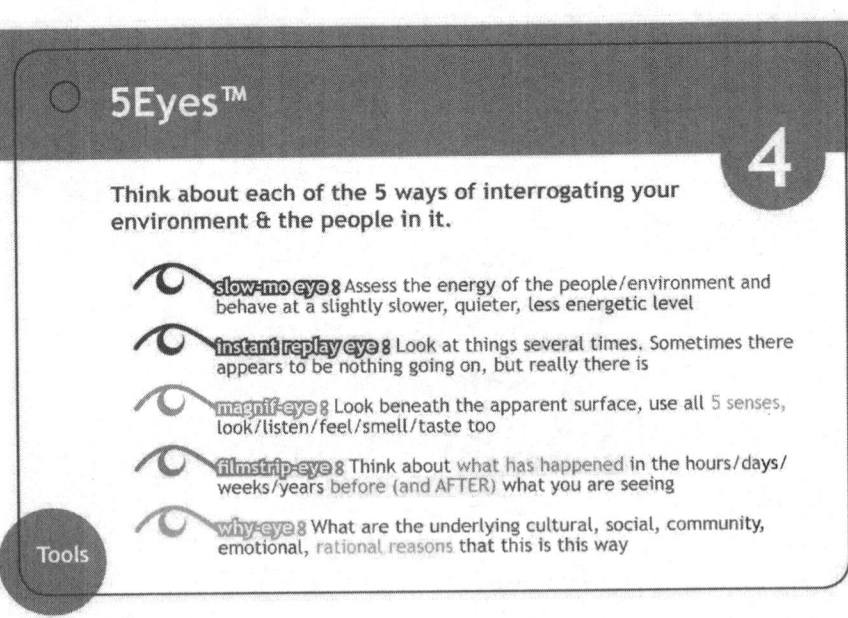

## 5Eyes™

**4**

**Think about each of the 5 ways of interrogating your environment & the people in it.**

**slow-mo eye :** Assess the energy of the people/environment and behave at a slightly slower, quieter, less energetic level

**instant replay eye :** Look at things several times. Sometimes there appears to be nothing going on, but really there is

**magnif-eye :** Look beneath the apparent surface, use all 5 senses, look/listen/feel/smell/taste too

**filmstrip-eye :** Think about what has happened in the hours/days/ weeks/years before (and AFTER) what you are seeing

**why-eye :** What are the underlying cultural, social, community, emotional, rational reasons that this is this way

Tools

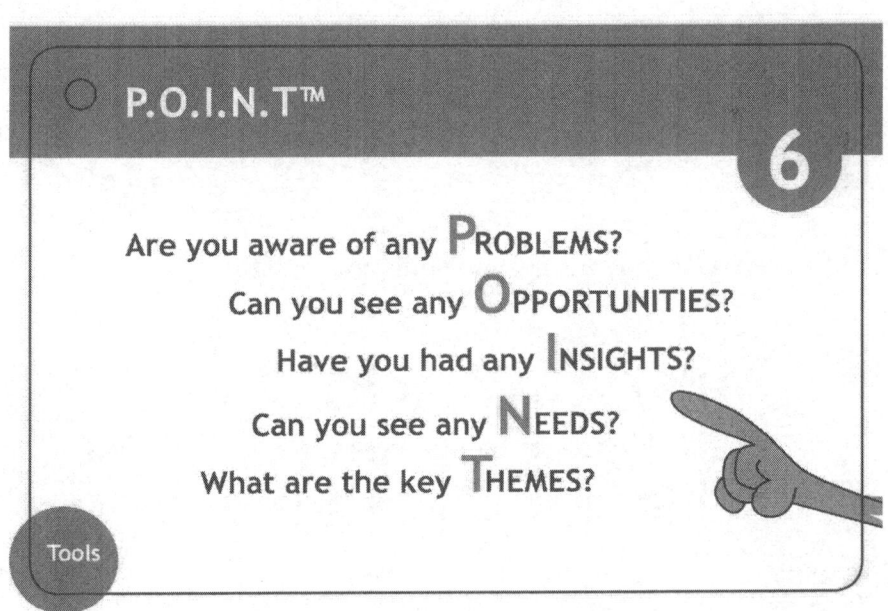

## Excursion Thinking

7

**Use other environments to stimulate ideas!**
How would we do this:

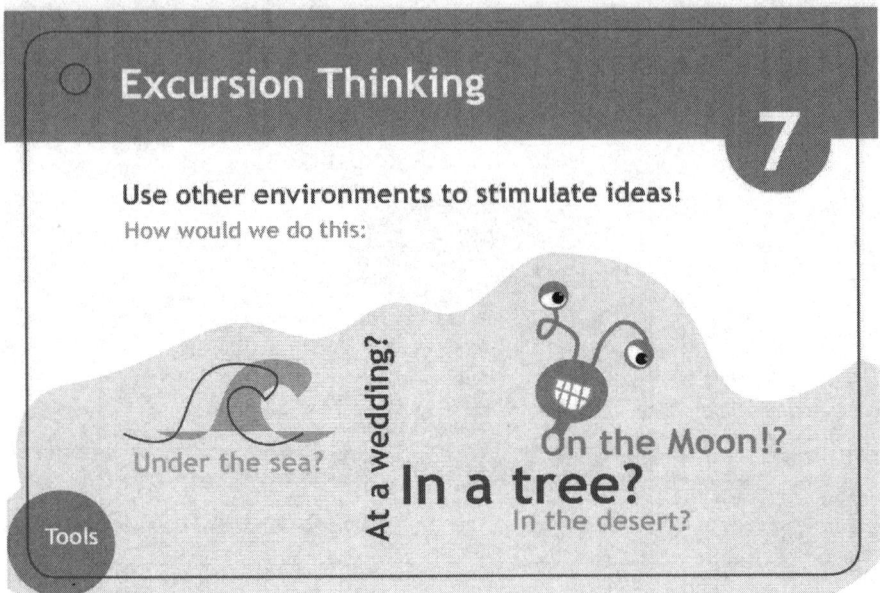

Under the sea?

At a wedding?

On the Moon!?

In a tree?

In the desert?

Tools

## Back-To-Front

8

Instead of trying to FIX problems...
Try to discover how you could make them
MUCH WORSE!

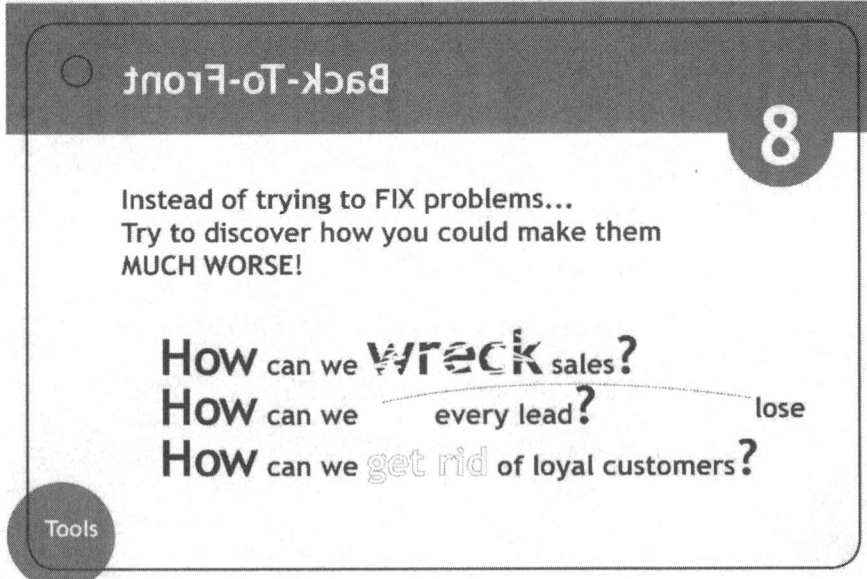

How can we wreck sales?

How can we every lead? lose

How can we get rid of loyal customers?

Tools

## Calling In Other Professionals

**9**

Think about your problem from the point of view of someone who is completely ignorant of the issue. How would your issue be tackled by:

# A hospi+al? A Publisher? The Police? The mafia?

Tools

## Random Connections

**10**

shrinking
placemat
idol purple
holding
doormat
dough
silence
angel nut
labrador
cowpat pretend
piglet
frantic
Ferrari
currency
interesting
planet
disguise
holiday.
therefore
waking
banana
cheque dragon
insect doing
sandwich random

Tools

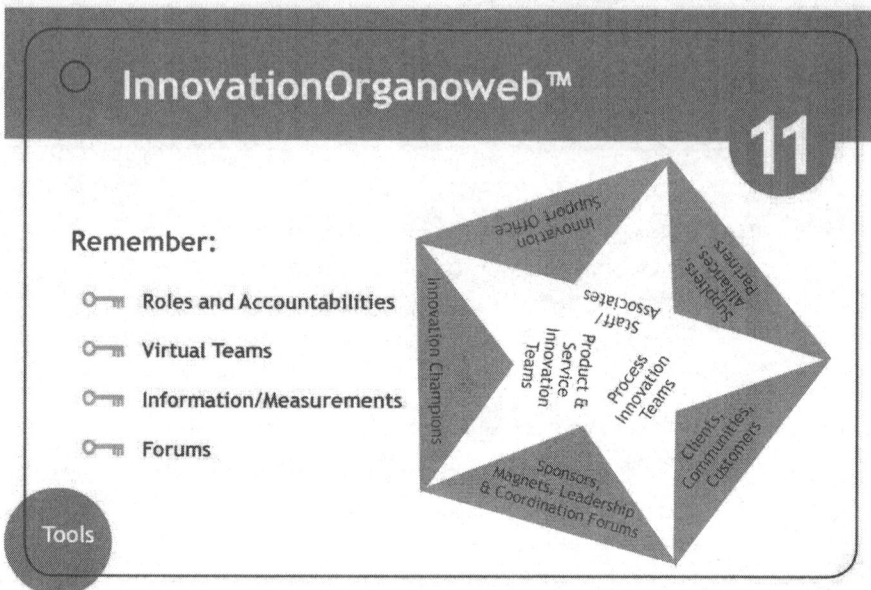

InnovationOrganoweb™

**11**

Remember:

- ⚷ Roles and Accountabilities
- ⚷ Virtual Teams
- ⚷ Information/Measurements
- ⚷ Forums

Innovation Support Office

Suppliers, Alliances, Partners

Innovation Champions

Staff/ Associates

Product & Service Innovation Teams

Process Innovation Teams

Clients, Communities, Customers

Sponsors, Magnets, Leadership & Coordination Forums

Tools

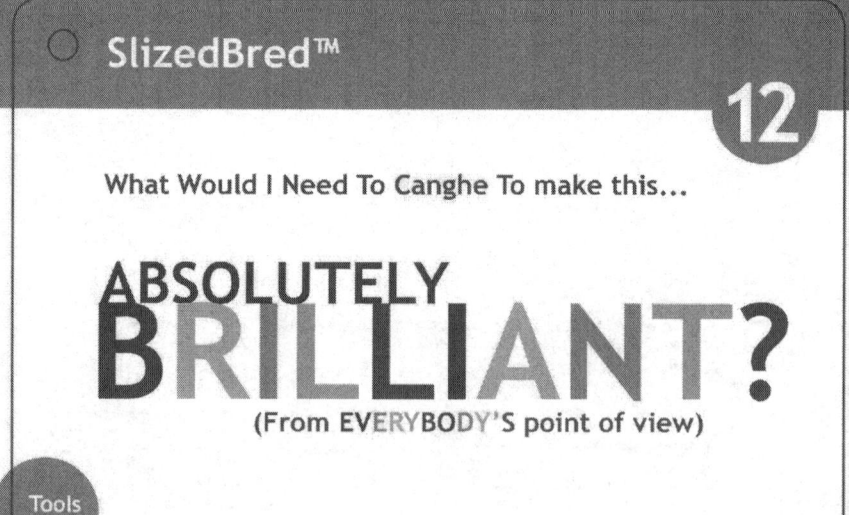

SlizedBred™

**12**

What Would I Need To Canghe To make this...

ABSOLUTELY
BRILLIANT?

(From EVERYBODY'S point of view)

Tools

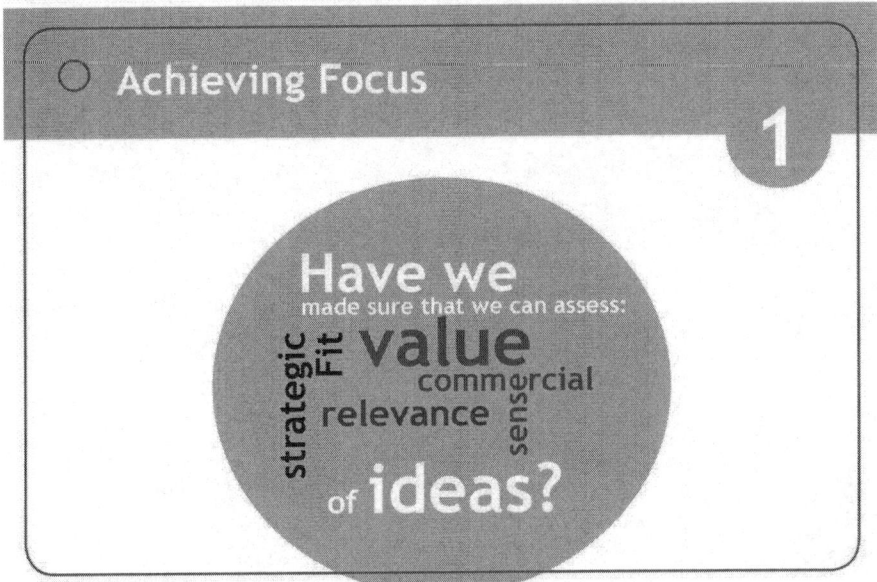

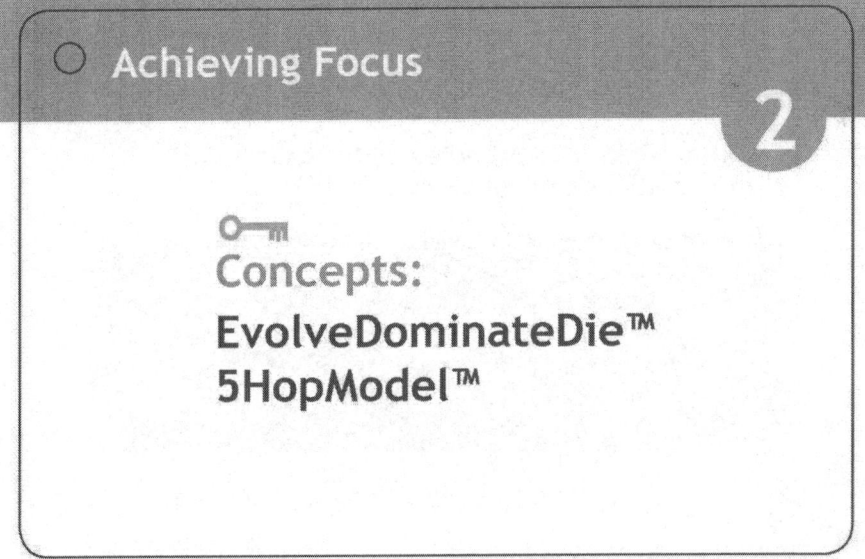

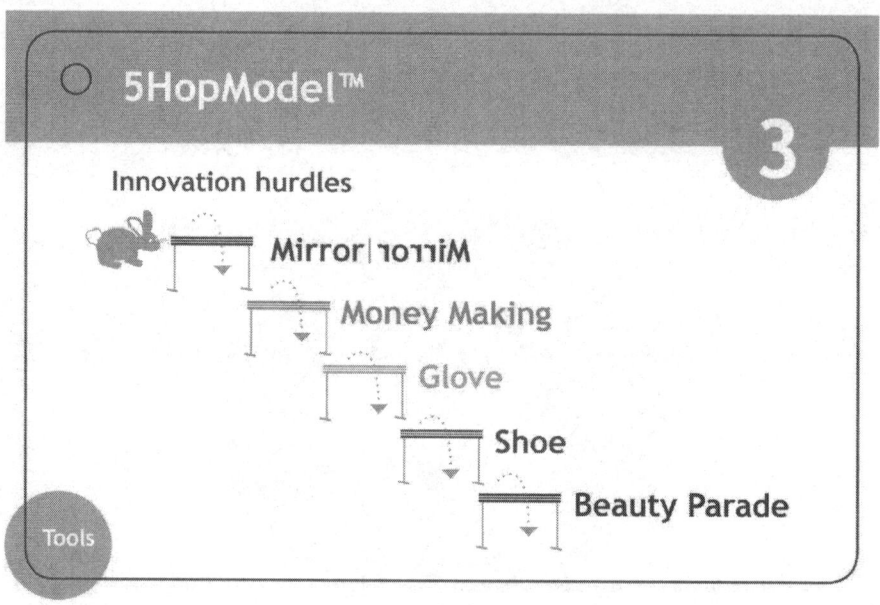

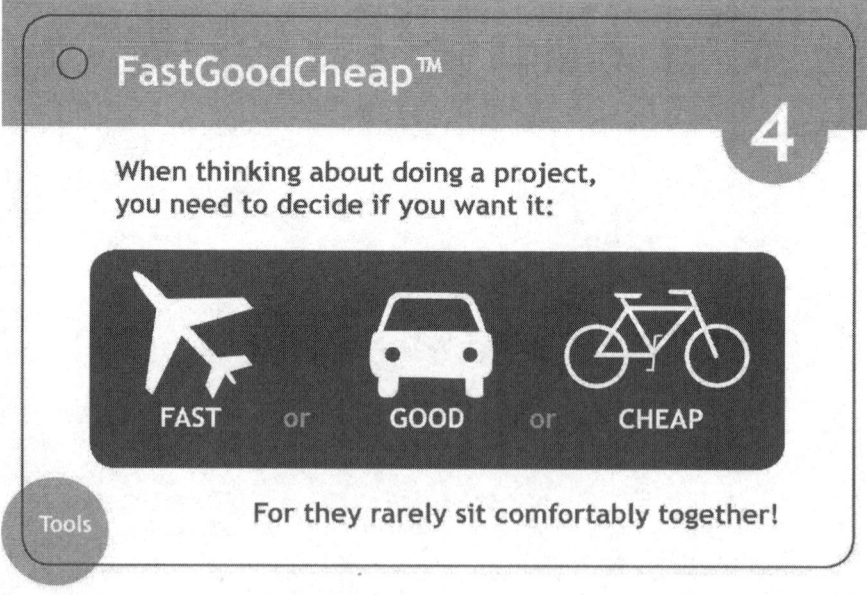

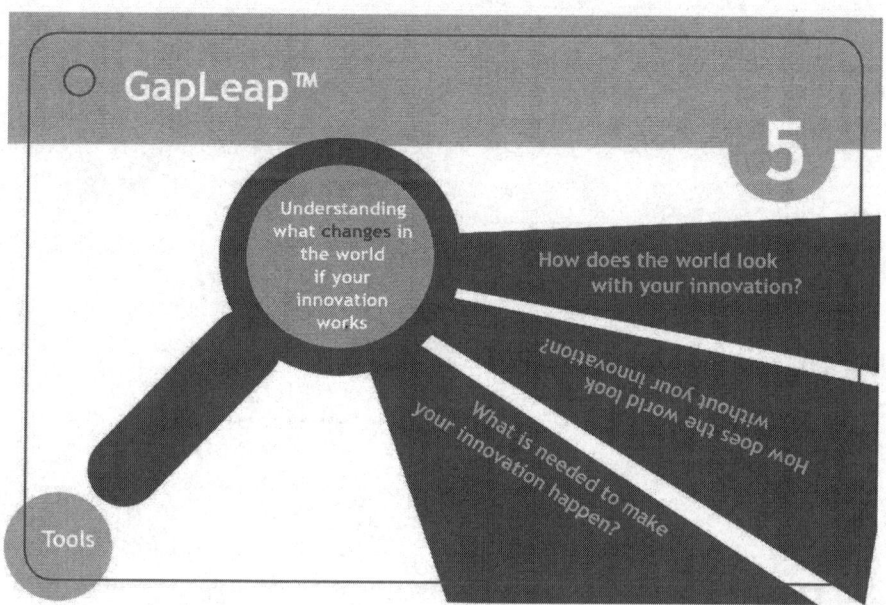

GapLeap™

5

Understanding what changes in the world if your innovation works

How does the world look with your innovation?

How does the world look without your innovation?

What is needed to make your innovation happen?

Tools

5 Reasons Strangers Give You Money

6

AURA

Risk Removal

Access

Tangibles

*i*nformatised Services

Tools

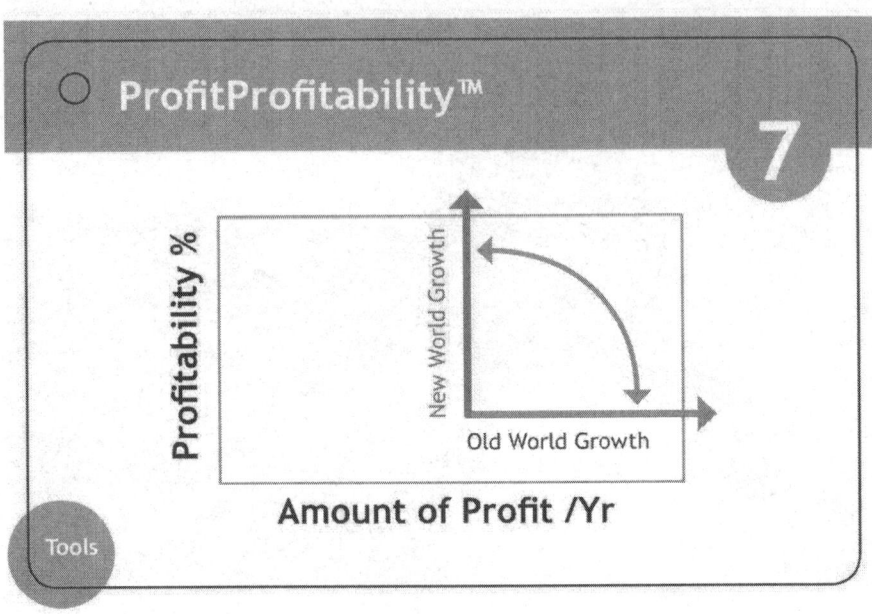

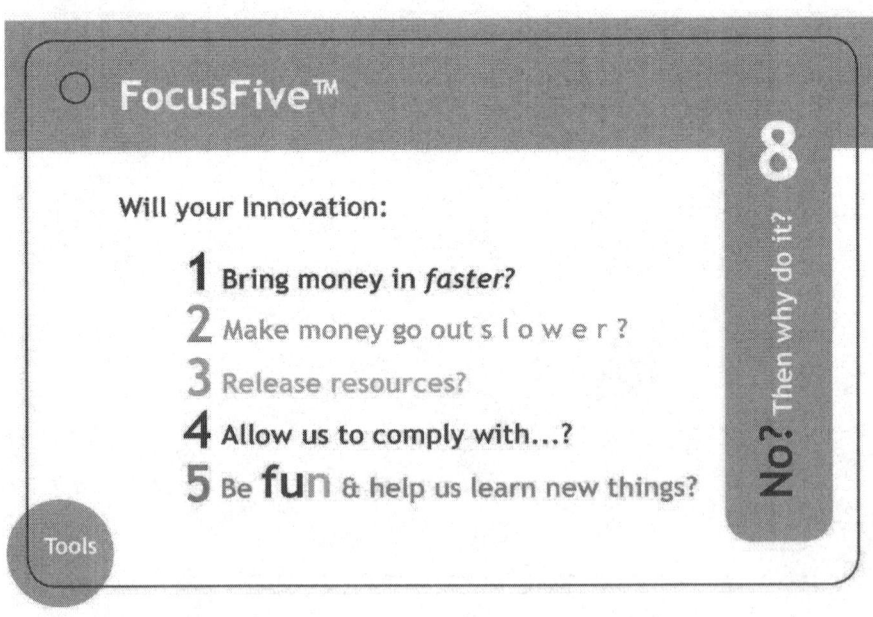

○ Anticip8™

9

What are the benefits of your
innovation on all levels?

HARD Soft
A.B.S.O.L.U.T.E.

Relative

Tools

## Engaging Commitment

**1**

## Have we:
removed all the
## barriers?
involved
all the right people?
## emotionally
prepared ourselves?

## Engaging Commitment

**2**

Concepts:

## Emotional Engagement
## Establishing Value

## Finding/Identifying Stakeholders

**3**

Give them reasons to bet on your success

Who can you do it without?

Who can you NOT do it without?

Who will be damaged by the project?

Who will benefit from the project?

Never surprise your stakeholders

**Tools**

Build trust rapidly to ensure they are really engaged

## Engaging Commitment

**4**

Who agrees with the goals?

Who does NOT agree with the goals?

Who understands what you are trying to achieve?

Who does NOT understand what you are trying to achieve?

Treat them accordingly

**Tools**

## Value Mapping

**5**

A way of clearly focusing priorities on activities which create real value.

**Activity does not always equal value.**

VALUE = BENEFITS - COSTS

Tools

## FutureFamiliar™

**6**

Make it Familiar.
Make it non-Threatening.

It's similar to...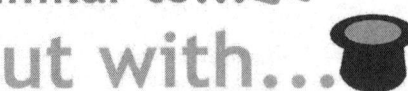

But with...

And what's REALLY great about it is...

Tools

## L-Eve-8™

**7**

### 30 Second Pitch
Make it familiar - Make it exciting!

It's like... Meets...

But without...

And what makes it REALLY cool is...

Tools

## IDQB™

**8**

PEOPLE CREATE CHANGE

PEOPLE CONSTRAIN CHANGE

Use to avoid resistance to change:

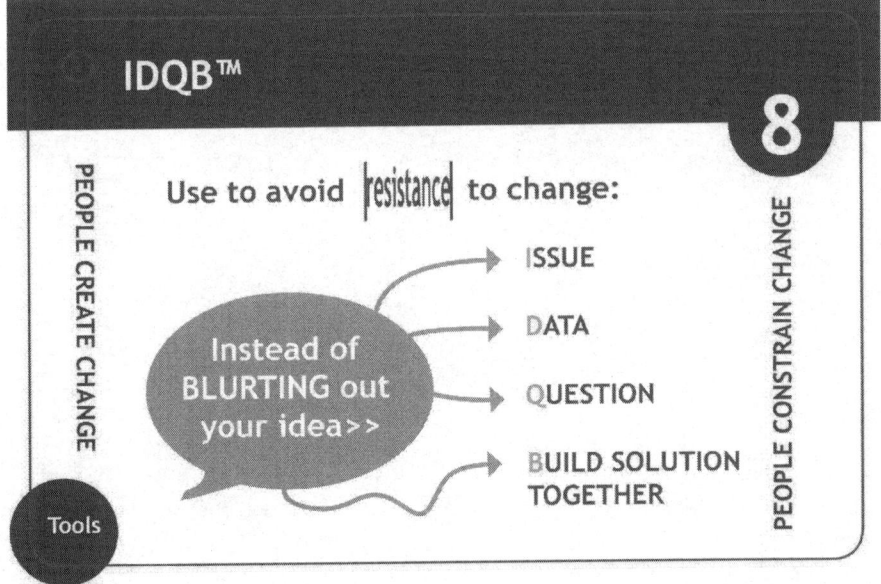

Instead of BLURTING out your idea>>

ISSUE

DATA

QUESTION

BUILD SOLUTION TOGETHER

Tools

## BlyndTrust™

**9**

**1** Promise it.

**2** Do it!

**3** **Remind** people you **promised it.**
**Remind** people you **did it!**

X **4 = TRUST!**

Tools

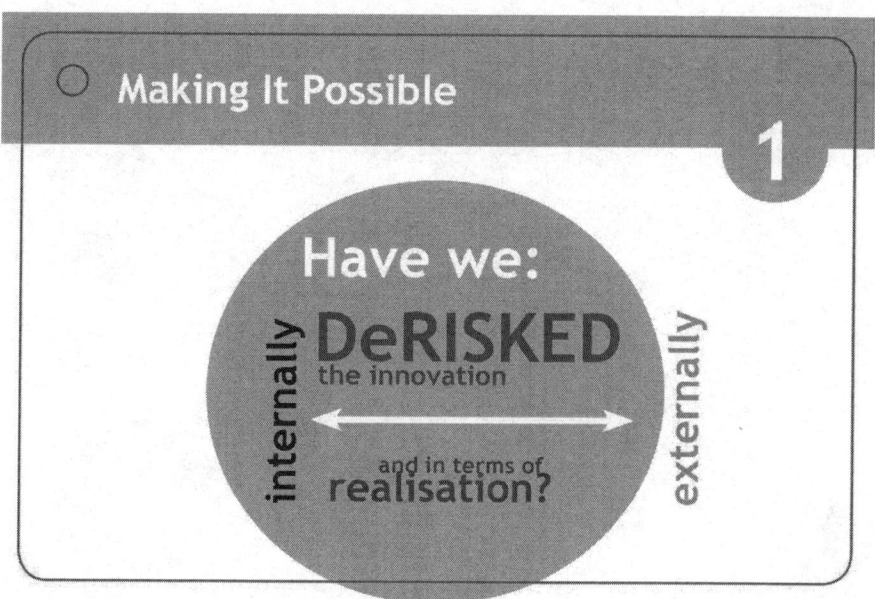

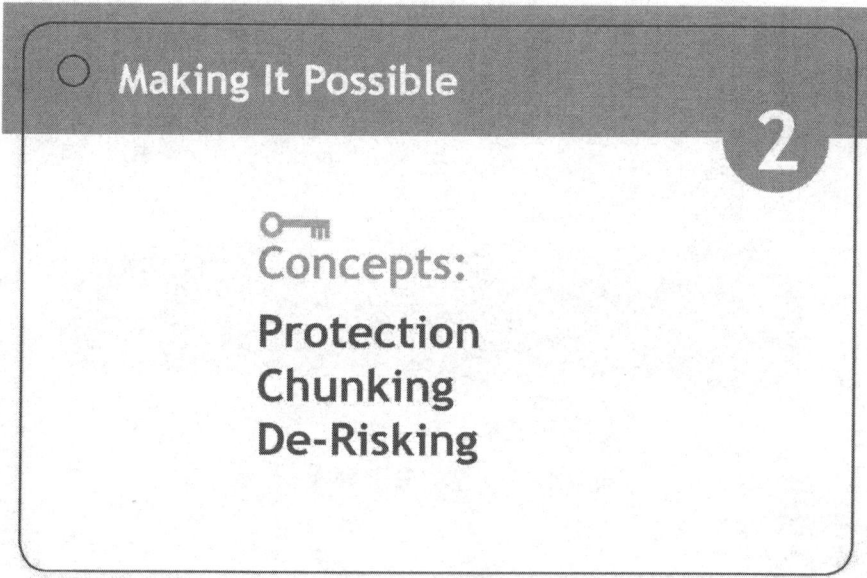

FixItNow™

3

Surviving the Alien invasion

1. List Fears
2. Kill them now!
3. Containment actions
What Fears are left?
4. Monitor them
5. Have a contingency/plan b

Tools

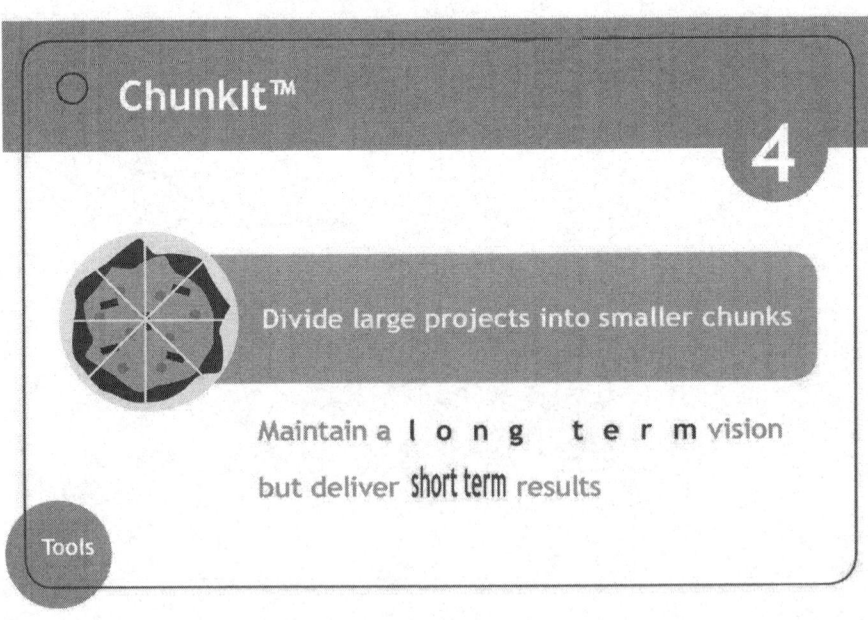

ChunkIt™

4

Divide large projects into smaller chunks

Maintain a **l o n g   t e r m** vision
but deliver **short term** results

Tools

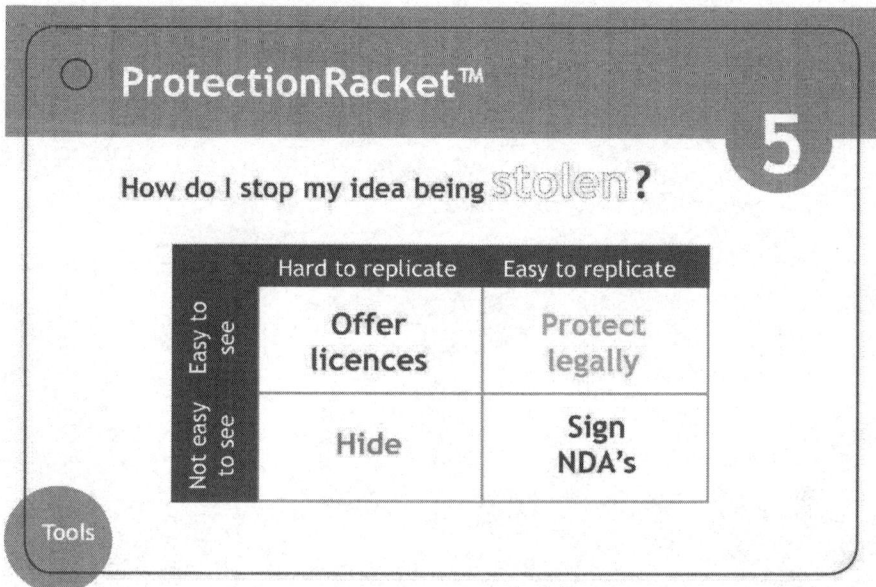

### ProtectionRacket™

**5**

How do I stop my idea being stolen?

| | Hard to replicate | Easy to replicate |
|---|---|---|
| Easy to see | **Offer licences** | Protect legally |
| Not easy to see | Hide | **Sign NDA's** |

Tools

### FutureMapping™

**6**

The future is an open book. ALWAYS read what happens NEXT!

My organisations responds by...
The regulator responds by...
The customers respond by...
My competitor responds by...

Tools

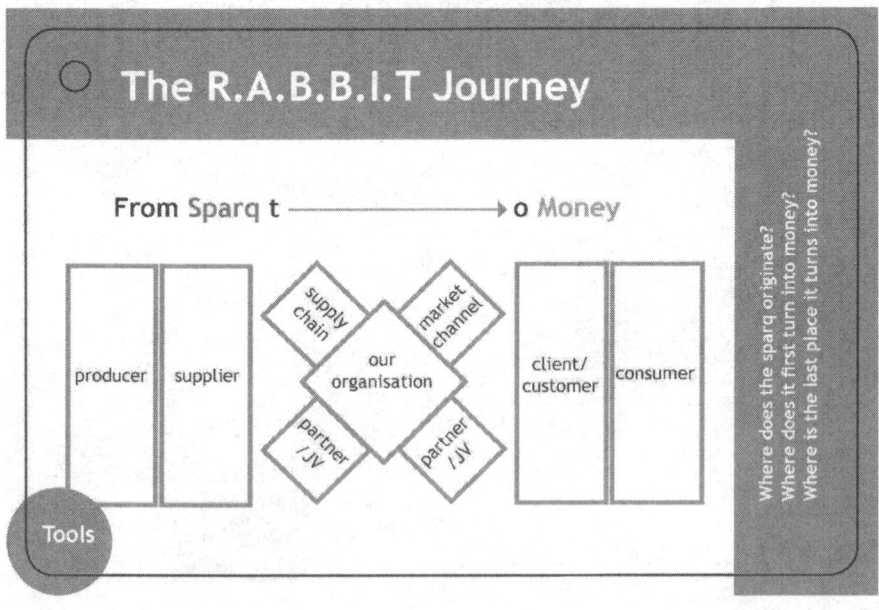

## Making It Happen

**1**

### Have we
Set up the:

right type
of project **4**

making money?

from the
innovation
/identifying
patterns

## Making It Happen

**2**

○━▥
Concepts:

**Project Types
Management Approach
Leadership**

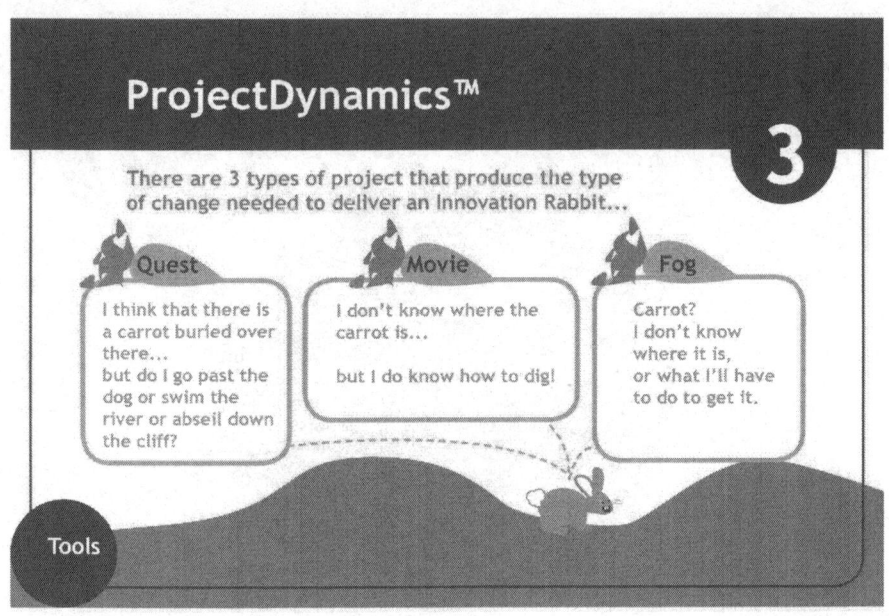

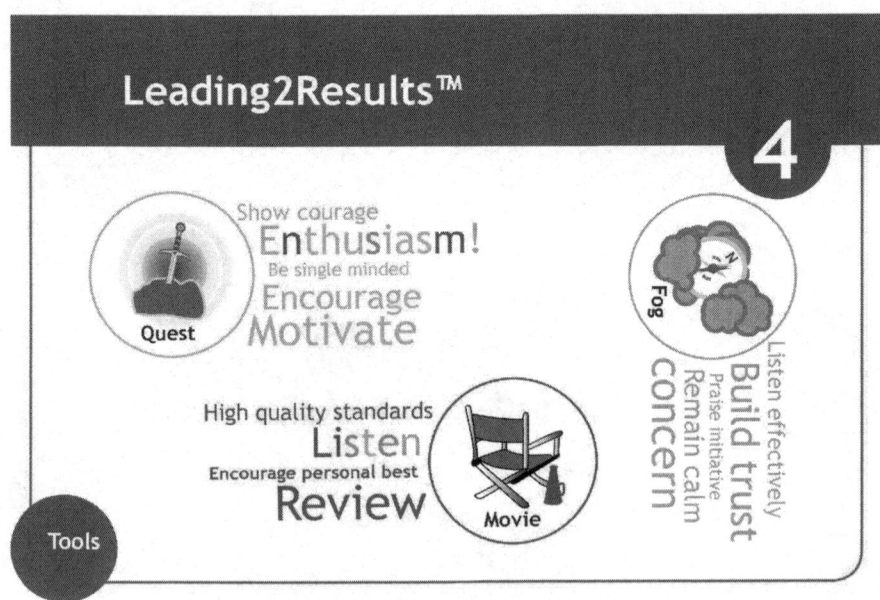

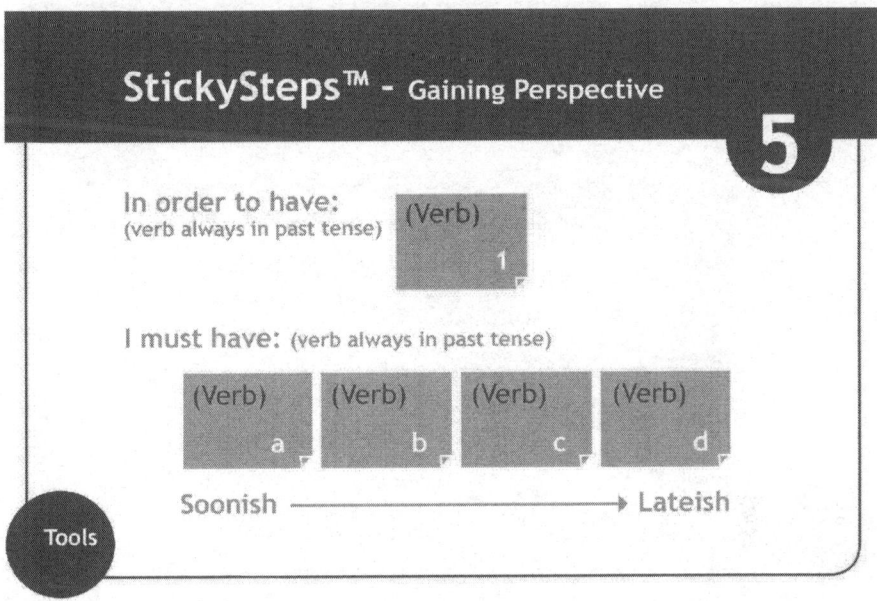

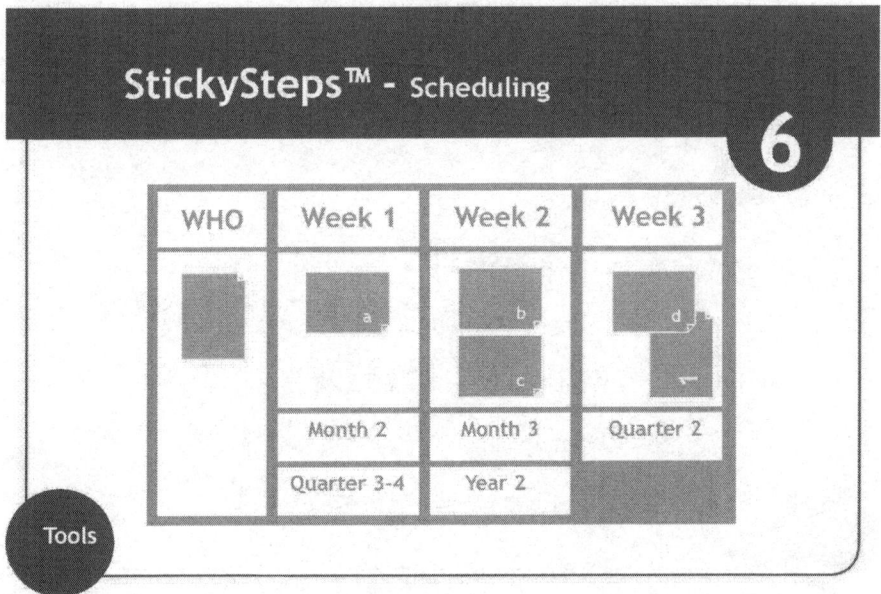

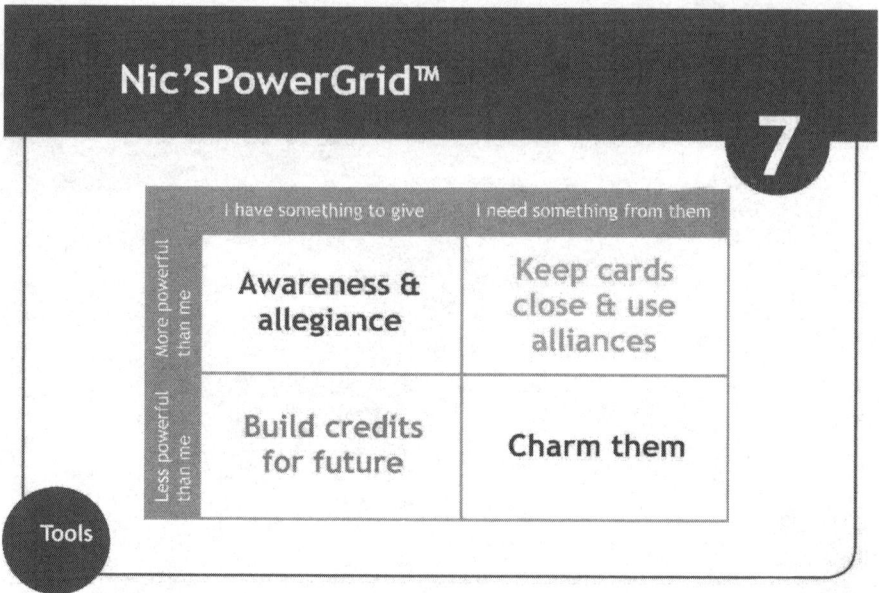

## Nic'sPowerGrid™

**7**

|  | I have something to give | I need something from them |
|---|---|---|
| **More powerful than me** | Awareness & allegiance | Keep cards close & use alliances |
| **Less powerful than me** | Build credits for future | Charm them |

Tools

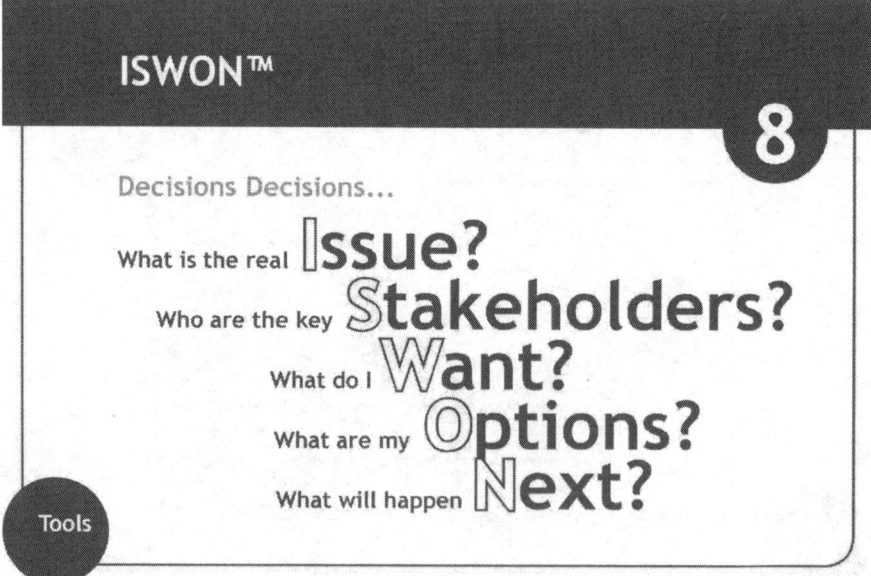

## ISWON™

**8**

Decisions Decisions...

What is the real **Issue?**

Who are the key **Stakeholders?**

What do I **Want?**

What are my **Options?**

What will happen **Next?**

Tools

## ActionReplay™

**9**

|  | Worked well? | Failed |
|---|---|---|
| **Planned?** | Why did it work?<br>How can we<br>do more? | Why did it fail?<br>What can we do<br>differently? |
| **Not planned?** | Why did this happen?<br>How can we<br>repeat it? | Why did this go<br>wrong?<br>How can we avoid it<br>next time? |

Tools

## The End

Focus on the biggest danger to save the most rabbits with the least effort and...

**...remember to nurture your rabbits**

**R.A.B.B.I.T**

**Eddie Obeng**
THE VIRTUAL BUSINESS SCHOOL

tel: +44 (0)1494 678555
email: RabbitCards@PentacleTheVBS.com
web: www.PentacleTheVBS.com

Card design by Ilona Plews

# PART THREE:
# THE EVIDENCE

PENTACLE RESEARCH METHOD: BUBBLEDIAGRAM[TM]

I am often asked why I have so few references in my books. Most people look for references to previous research or the comfort and reassurance of a well-known publisher as a way to tell if a book can be trusted or not. Good stuff, but from the world before midnight.

So let me explain the **Pentacle Research Method**.

What is your reaction to these statements?

'We interviewed 1200 chief executives and discovered that 87% of them stated that weak innovation was their main challenge.'

'We analysed 3 similar cases (and were successful in predicting 3 further cases in detail from our model) which demonstrate a complex but clear, strong pattern of how innovation is blocked.'

Which do you see as better research – the sort of thing you would bet your company on?

Science was once about 'Why?' Why don't we fall off the earth? Why does a feather fall at the same speed as a lead plate in a vacuum? Why do similar birds from different islands have different beaks? From these deep, profound 'Why?' questions we observed diligently, made discoveries and founded laws based on the repetitiveness of patterns. In science after 'Why?' came 'How?'

And then the age of mumbo jumbo[9] dawned: we moved from facts, proof and experiment to opinion, views and belief – where everyone's opinion was as good as everyone else's and as long as you sincerely and strongly held your belief you didn't have to apologise for it even if it was patently nonsense. The doctrine of pre-emption suggested you should act to prevent what hadn't happened and for which there was no evidence that it would ever happen… And we harnessed the number crunching capability of computers. Suddenly we no longer asked 'Why?' but 'What?' What do celebrities think of plastic surgery? There has been a 20-point rise in the FTSE. Crime is going down – reported crime rates have fallen by 2%. All pointless statements without the appropriate relative measures or statistical analysis. And yet statements typical of modern news reporting. What's the year-on-year standard

---

9    Francis Wheen (2004) *How Mumbo Jumbo Conquered the World*. London: HarperCollins.

deviation for the crime statistics? What are the control limits? Is there really a downward trend? But most importantly, if there really is a downward trend, **why is it happening** and **how** do we make it go faster?

Occasionally we ask 'How?' A strong pound has reduced the demand for oil. The late departure of your flight is because of the late arrival of the aircraft – due to technical problems!

'How?' without 'Why?' is like witchcraft. **Solutions without understanding**. How do you get your Presidential approval ratings up? You have a (short) war. But if you don't understand why it works you may discover that it doesn't.

In a world where you could learn faster than things are changing around you it was a bit dangerous but acceptable to take this path. Tomorrow looked like today and extrapolation was a great idea.

However, we now live in a new world – one where change can outstrip your ability to learn. In this world, events change rapidly – but fortunately the underlying structures and patterns change more slowly. Events evaporate but patterns persist and sustainable business success is based on patterns not events.

| State | TRADITIONAL OLD WORLD | COMPLEX, CHANGING NEW WORLD | COMPLEX, CHANGING NEW WORLD |
|---|---|---|---|
| | | Right Response | Wrong Response |
| **Tools** | Incidence, distribution and correlation | Causality and prediction | Hunches, unfounded 'what ifs' |
| **Approach** | Large samples give credibility | Small samples and regular review give credibility | Dinner conversations with like-minded people |

## How do you do your research so fast?

*Home grown, tried and tested!*

*In a world that changes fast our research needs to be faster!*

Step 1 - Find Cases where outcome is unexpected and repeated

Step 2 - Interview people involved to determine '**causality**'. Traditional 'Old World' research looks for distribution ("70% of CEO's said...") and correlation ("as the Pound Sterling becomes stronger the level of exports has fallen"). Interesting trivia but it doesn't pin-point what to do about it

Step 3
Turn **causality** links into a Bubble Diagram™

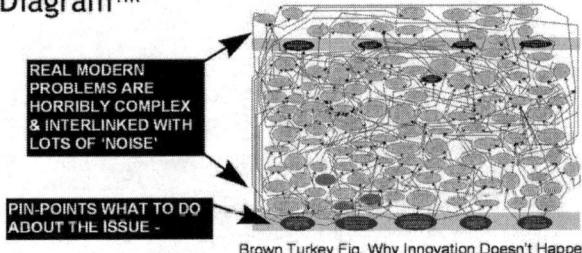

REAL MODERN PROBLEMS ARE HORRIBLY COMPLEX & INTERLINKED WITH LOTS OF 'NOISE'

PIN-POINTS WHAT TO DO ABOUT THE ISSUE -

Brown Turkey Fig. Why Innovation Doesn't Happen

Step 4 Interview more people and other cases looking for omissions and inconsistencies in the Bubble Diagram™

Step 5 Use the Bubble Diagram™ for prediction - If someone says they have an issue use the Bubble Diagram™ to pinpoint future issues and events and check if your predictions come true

PENTACLE

PENTACLE HUB-Q AND CONTACT DETAILS

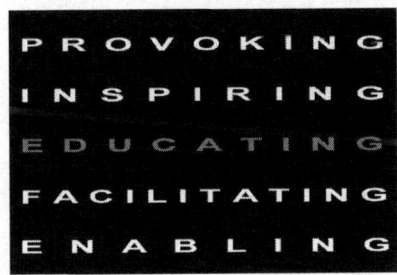

## PENTACLE Learning2Transform:

You can webmail us:  here
Email us at:  Admin@PentacleTheVBS.com
Phone us (24h) on:  +441494678555  http://QUBE.cc:
Maps are available:  here

Fax us at:  +44 (0) 1494671291

At any time you can enter the *qubicles* where much of the action in the book takes place. Invite a couple of your colleagues to join you in the qubicle and try out some of the tools and techniques together.

Project qubicle here: ♣

Innovation Workshop Qubicle here: ♣

♣Access to QUBE:

Your user name is: me<use a number from 1 to 100>@ALCORP. com  For example me57@alcorp.com

Your password is Sparq. <capital S>

Join the WAM innovation community in hub-Q. Apply for an entry pass and get details of the amazing 'Introductory Offer'! http://hub-Q.com

## *Image acknowledgements*

Chapter 1 opening: Lightning (j_arred)
Chapter 2 opening: Present (S Baker)
Chapter 3 opening: Not the Comfy Chair! (alexbrn)
Chapter 4 opening: Geranium pot (Robyn Jay)
Chapter 5 opening: Invicta 8926 closeup (Bill Bradford)
Chapter 6 opening: Old map (Enrique Flouret)
Chapter 7 opening: Seal pup (courtesy of Dr. Brandon Southall, NMFS/OPR)
Chapter 8 opening: Justice (Mike Gifford)
Chapter 9 opening: Clothing factory (Edwin Lee)
Chapter 10 opening: Not my hat! (Alan Levine)
Chapter 11 opening: Chess Pieces (Tom Von Lahndorff)
Chapter 12 opening: Just a Brick Wall (Jayel Aheram)
Chapter 13 opening: Magazine Stand (Tracy Hunter)
Chapter 14 opening: Hokus (Jennifer Morton)
Chapter 15 opening: Mirror Ball Amsterdam (Ewan Topping)
Chapter 16 opening: Zebras (Corey Leopold)
Chapter 17 opening: Tug of War... (Steven Guzzardi)
Chapter 18 opening: Whodunnit (Gordon Joly)